GLENCOE LANGUAGE ARTS

VOCABULARY POWER

GRADE 12

Glencoe McGraw-Hill

New York, New York   Columbus, Ohio   Woodland Hills, California   Peoria, Illinois

To the Student

This *Vocabulary Power* workbook gives you the practice you need to expand your vocabulary and improve your ability to understand what you read. Each lesson focuses on a single vocabulary concept or on a theme that ties together the list of words in the Word Bank. You then have several opportunities to learn the words by completing exercises on definitions, context clues, and word parts.

You can keep track of your own progress and achievement in vocabulary study by using the Student Progress Chart, which appears on page v. With your teacher's help, you can score your work on any lesson or test. After you know your score, use the Scoring Scale on pages vi–vii to figure your percentage. Then mark your score (or percentage correct) on the Student Progress Chart. Share your Progress Chart with your parents or guardians as your teacher directs.

Glencoe/McGraw-Hill

A Division of The McGraw·Hill Companies

Send all inquiries to:
Glencoe/McGraw-Hill
8787 Orion Place
Columbus, Ohio 43240

ISBN 0-07-826236-4

Printed in the United States of America

1 2 3 4 5 6 7 8 9 10 024 05 04 03 02 01

CONTENTS

Student Progress Chart v
Scoring Scale vi

Unit 1
Lesson 1   Dictionary Definitions 1
Lesson 2   Using Synonyms and Antonyms 3
Lesson 3   Base Words and Word Roots 5
Lesson 4   Using Reading Skills—Learning from Context: Definitions 7
Review 8
Test 9

Unit 2
Lesson 5   Dictionary Definitions 11
Lesson 6   Word Families 13
Lesson 7   Connotation and Denotation 15
Lesson 8   Using Reference Skills—Using a Dictionary: Word Origins 17
Review 18
Test 19

Unit 3
Lesson 9   Using Synonyms 21
Lesson 10   Word Roots *terr*, *lun*, and *astr* 23
Lesson 11   Prefixes That Show Negation 25
Lesson 12   Using Reading Skills—Learning from Context 27
Review 28
Test 29

Unit 4
Lesson 13   Word Usage 31
Lesson 14   Suffixes That Form Nouns 33
Lesson 15   Prefixes That Show Direction or Position 35
Lesson 16   Using Reference Skills—Using a Thesaurus: Synonyms and Antonyms 37
Review 38
Test 39

Unit 5
Lesson 17   Using Synonyms 41
Lesson 18   The Word Roots *morph*, *flu/fluct/flux*, *tact/tang/tig*, *prehend/prehens* 43
Lesson 19   The Prefixes *im-*, *in-*, and *un-* 45
Lesson 20   Using Reference Skills—Using a Dictionary: Multiple-Meaning Words 47
Review 48
Test 49

Unit 6
Lesson 21   Using Synonyms 51
Lesson 22   Suffixes That Form Adjectives 53
Lesson 23   The Word Roots *cred*, *ten* 55
Lesson 24   Using Reading Skills—Learning from Context: Comparison and Contrast . . .57
Review 58
Test 59

Unit 7

Lesson 25	Word Usage	.61
Lesson 26	Word Root *gen*	.63
Lesson 27	The Prefix *trans-*	.65
Lesson 28	Using Reading Skills—Learning from Context	.67
Review		.68
Test		.69

Unit 8

Lesson 29	Using Context Clues	.71
Lesson 30	Base Words	.73
Lesson 31	The Greek Root *graph/gram*	.75
Lesson 32	Using Reference Skills—Antonyms	.77
Review		.78
Test		.79

Unit 9

Lesson 33	Using Synonyms	.81
Lesson 34	Prefixes Meaning "for" and "against"	.83
Lesson 35	The Greek Root *bio* and the Latin Root *vit*	.85
Lesson 36	Using Test-Taking Skills—Analogies	.87
Review		.88
Test		.89

Unit 10

Lesson 37	Word Definitions	.91
Lesson 38	The Greek Roots *phos* and *phot* and the Latin Root *luc*	.93
Lesson 39	The Latin Root *memor* and Prefix *retro-*	.95
Lesson 40	Using Test-Taking Skills—Sentence Completion	.97
Review		.98
Test		.99

Unit 11

Lesson 41	Using Context Clues	.101
Lesson 42	Using Synonyms	.103
Lesson 43	The Latin Root *ludus*	.105
Review		.107
Test		.108

Unit 12

Lesson 44	Word Usage	.110
Lesson 45	Prefixes That Show Quantity or Size	.112
Lesson 46	Words from Technology	.114
Review		.116
Test		.117

Pronunciation Guide .119

STUDENT PROGRESS CHART

Fill in the chart below with your scores, using the scoring scale on the next page.

Name: _____

	Lesson	Unit Review	Unit Test
1			
2			
3			
4			
Review			
Test			
5			
6			
7			
8			
Review			
Test			
9			
10			
11			
12			
Review			
Test			
13			
14			
15			
16			
Review			
Test			
17			
18			
19			
20			
Review			
Test			
21			
22			
23			
24			
Review			
Test			
25			
26			
27			
28			
Review			
Test			
29			
30			
31			
32			
Review			
Test			
33			
34			
35			
36			
Review			
Test			
37			
38			
39			
40			
Review			
Test			
41			
42			
43			
Review			
Test			
44			
45			
46			
Review			
Test			

SCORING SCALE

Use this scale to find your score. Line up the number of items with the number correct. For example, if 15 out of 16 items are correct, the score is 93.7 percent (see grayed area).

Number Correct

Number of Items	1	2	3	4	5	6	7	8	9	10	11	12	13	14	15	16	17	18	19	20
1	100																			
2	50	100																		
3	33.3	66.7	100																	
4	25	50	75	100																
5	20	40	60	80	100															
6	16.7	33.3	50	66.7	83.3	100														
7	14.3	28.6	42.9	57.1	71.4	85.7	100													
8	12.5	25	37.5	50	62.5	75	87.5	100												
9	11.1	22.2	33.3	44.4	55.6	66.7	77.8	88.9	100											
10	10	20	30	40	50	60	70	80	90	100										
11	9.1	18.1	27.2	36.3	45.4	54.5	63.6	72.7	81.8	90.9	100									
12	8.3	16.7	25	33.3	41.7	50	58.3	66.7	75	83.3	91.7	100								
13	7.7	15.3	23.1	30.8	38.5	46.1	53.8	61.5	69.2	76.9	84.6	92.3	100							
14	7.1	14.3	21.4	28.6	35.7	42.8	50	57.1	64.3	71.4	78.5	85.7	92.8	100						
15	6.7	13.3	20	26.7	33.3	40	46.6	53.3	60	66.7	73.3	80	86.7	93.3	100					
16	6.3	12.5	18.8	25	31.2	37.5	43.7	50	56.2	62.5	68.7	75	81.2	87.5	93.7	100				
17	5.9	11.8	17.6	23.5	29.4	35.3	41.2	47	52.9	58.8	64.7	70.6	76.5	82.3	88.2	94.1	100			
18	5.6	11.1	16.7	22.2	27.8	33.3	38.9	44.4	50	55.5	61.1	66.7	72.2	77.8	83.3	88.9	94.4	100		
19	5.3	10.5	15.8	21.2	26.3	31.6	36.8	42.1	47.4	52.6	57.9	63.1	68.4	73.7	78.9	84.2	89.4	94.7	100	
20	5	10	15	20	25	30	35	40	45	50	55	60	65	70	85	80	85	90	95	100
21	4.8	9.5	14.3	19	23.8	28.6	33.3	38.1	42.8	47.6	52.3	57.1	61.9	66.7	71.4	76.1	80.9	85.7	90.5	95.2
22	4.5	9.1	13.7	18.2	22.7	27.3	31.8	36.4	40.9	45.4	50	54.5	59.1	63.6	68.1	72.7	77.2	81.8	86.4	90.9
23	4.3	8.7	13.0	17.4	21.7	26.1	30.4	34.8	39.1	43.5	47.8	52.1	56.5	60.8	65.2	69.5	73.9	78.3	82.6	86.9
24	4.7	8.3	12.5	16.7	20.8	25	29.2	33.3	37.5	41.7	45.8	50	54.2	58.3	62.5	66.7	70.8	75	79.1	83.3
25	4	8	12	16	20	24	28	32	36	40	44	48	52	56	60	64	68	72	76	80
26	3.8	7.7	11.5	15.4	19.2	23.1	26.9	30.4	34.6	38.5	42.3	46.2	50	53.8	57.7	61.5	65.4	69.2	73.1	76.9
27	3.7	7.4	11.1	14.8	18.5	22.2	25.9	29.6	33.3	37	40.7	44.4	48.1	51.9	55.6	59.2	63	66.7	70.4	74.1
28	3.6	7.1	10.7	14.3	17.9	21.4	25	28.6	32.1	35.7	39.3	42.9	46.4	50	53.6	57.1	60.7	64.3	67.9	71.4
29	3.4	6.9	10.3	13.8	17.2	20.7	24.1	27.6	31	34.5	37.9	41.4	44.8	48.3	51.7	55.2	58.6	62.1	65.5	69
30	3.3	6.7	10	13.3	16.7	20	23.3	26.7	30	33.3	36.7	40	43.3	46.7	50	53.3	56.7	60	63.3	66.7
31	3.2	6.5	9.7	13	16.1	19.3	22.3	25.8	29.0	32.2	35.4	38.7	41.9	45.1	48.3	51.6	54.8	58	61.2	64.5
32	3.1	6.3	9.4	12.5	15.6	18.8	21.9	25	28.1	31.3	34.4	37.5	40.6	43.8	46.9	50	53.1	56.2	59.4	62.5
33	3	6	9	12	15.1	18.1	21.2	24.2	27.2	30.3	33	36.3	39.3	42.4	45.4	48.4	51.5	54.5	57.5	60.6
34	2.9	5.9	8.8	11.8	14.7	17.6	20.6	23.5	26.5	29.4	32.4	35.3	38.2	41.2	44.1	47.1	50	52.9	55.9	58.8
35	2.9	5.7	8.6	11.4	14.3	17.1	20	22.9	25.7	28.6	31.4	34.3	37.1	40	42.9	45.7	48.6	51.4	54.3	57.1
36	2.8	5.6	8.3	11.1	13.9	16.7	19.4	22.2	25	27.8	30.6	33.3	36.1	38.9	41.7	44.4	47.2	50	52.7	55.6
37	2.7	5.4	8.1	10.8	13.5	17.1	18.9	21.6	24.3	27	29.7	32.4	35.1	37.8	40	43.2	45.9	48.6	51.4	54
38	2.6	5.3	7.9	10.5	13.2	15.8	18.4	21.1	23.7	26.3	28.9	31.6	34.2	36.8	39.5	42.1	44.7	47.4	50	52.6
39	2.6	5.3	7.7	10.3	12.8	15.4	17.9	20.5	23.1	25.6	28.2	30.8	33.3	35.9	38.5	41.0	43.6	46.2	48.7	51.3
40	2.5	5	7.5	10	12.5	15	17.5	20	22.5	25	27.5	30	32.5	35	37.5	40	42.5	45	47.5	50

Number Correct

Number of Items	21	22	23	24	25	26	27	28	29	30	31	32	33	34	35	36	37	38	39	40
1																				
2																				
3																				
4																				
5																				
6																				
7																				
8																				
9																				
10																				
11																				
12																				
13																				
14																				
15																				
16																				
17																				
18																				
19																				
20																				
21	100																			
22	95.4	100																		
23	91.3	95.6	100																	
24	87.5	91.6	95.8	100																
25	84	88	92	96	100															
26	80.8	84.6	88.5	92.3	96.2	100														
27	77.8	81.5	85.2	88.9	92.6	96.3	100													
28	75	78.6	82.1	85.7	89.3	92.9	96.4	100												
29	72.4	75.9	79.3	82.8	86.2	89.7	93.1	96.6	100											
30	70	73.3	76.7	80	83.3	86.7	90	93.3	96.7	100										
31	67.7	70.9	74.2	77.4	80.6	83.9	87.1	90.3	93.5	96.7	100									
32	65.6	68.8	71.9	75	78.1	81.2	84.4	87.5	90.6	93.8	96.9	100								
33	63.6	66.7	69.7	72.7	75.8	78.8	81.8	84.8	87.8	90.9	93.9	96.9	100							
34	61.8	64.7	67.6	70.6	73.5	76.5	79.3	82.4	85.3	88.2	91.2	94.1	97.1	100						
35	60	62.9	65.7	68.9	71.4	74.3	77.1	80	82.9	85.7	88.6	91.4	94.3	97.1	100					
36	58.3	61.1	63.8	66.7	69.4	72.2	75	77.8	80.6	85.7	86.1	88.9	91.7	94.9	97.2	100				
37	56.8	59.5	62.2	64.9	67.6	70.3	72.9	75.7	78.4	81.1	83.8	86.5	89.2	91.9	94.6	97.3	100			
38	55.3	57.9	60.5	63.2	65.8	68.4	71.2	73.7	76.3	78.9	81.6	84.2	86.8	89.5	92.1	94.7	97.3	100		
39	53.8	56.4	58.9	61.5	64.1	66.7	69.2	71.8	74.4	76.9	79.5	82.1	84.6	87.2	89.7	92.3	94.9	97.4	100	
40	52.5	55	57.5	60	62.5	65	67.5	70	72.5	75	77.5	80	82.5	85	87.5	90	92.5	95	97.5	100

Vocabulary Power

Lesson 1   Dictionary Definitions

Sometimes there is little difference between the heroes and the humble. The same personal qualities that serve the hero also help the humble meet life's everyday challenges. This lesson contains words you can use to discuss the heroic and the humble.

Word List

adversary	furtive	nullify	pensive
burgeoning	gallant	parry	respite
diligently	lurid		

EXERCISE A   Synonyms

Synonyms are words with similar meanings. Each boldfaced word below is paired with a synonym whose meaning you probably know. Think of other words related to the synonym and write them on the line provided. Then, look up the word in a dictionary and write its meaning.

1. **pensive** : thoughtful _____

    Dictionary definition _____

2. **diligently** : thoroughly _____

    Dictionary definition _____

3. **parry** : deflect _____

    Dictionary definition _____

4. **gallant** : brave _____

    Dictionary definition _____

5. **nullify** : neutralize _____

    Dictionary definition _____

6. **respite** : period of rest _____

    Dictionary definition _____

7. **lurid** : ghastly _____

    Dictionary definition _____

8. **adversary** : enemy _____

    Dictionary definition _____

9. **burgeoning** : expanding _____

    Dictionary definition _____

10. **furtive** : sly _____

    Dictionary definition _____

Vocabulary Power *continued*

EXERCISE B Word Meanings

Answer each question.

1. In your opinion, why do some newspapers and television news shows feature **lurid** stories?

   _____

2. Who is the most **pensive** person you know? Do you like this characteristic? Why or why not?

   _____

3. Name a **gallant** character from literature or movies. What do you like about this character?

   _____

4. Which school is your school's most important **adversary** in basketball, soccer, or football? Why is this rivalry the biggest?

   _____

5. Do you think violence in TV, movies, and video games is responsible for what some people believe is the **burgeoning** crime rate among youth? Why or why not?

   _____

6. How does a **respite** from studying improve your productivity?

   _____

EXERCISE C Multiple-Meaning Words

Many words have more than one meaning. The words *gallant* and *lurid* have several different meanings. Look these words up in a dictionary and, on a separate sheet of paper, write five sentences using a different meaning of these words in each sentence. After each sentence, write the definition you used.

Vocabulary Power

Lesson 2 Using Synonyms and Antonyms

Many different qualities can describe heroism and humility, just as many experiences cause human beings to act with heroism or humility. The following words are related to the heroic and the humble.

Word List

copiously	mollify	poignant	steadfastly
deftly	parch	solicitous	writhe
gullible	pernicious		

EXERCISE A Synonyms

Each boldfaced word below is paired with a synonym whose meaning you probably know. For each pair, think of other words related to the synonym and write them on the line provided. Then, look up the word in a dictionary and write its meaning.

1. **parch** : dry out _____

   Dictionary definition _____

2. **mollify** : soothe _____

   Dictionary definition _____

3. **poignant** : touching _____

   Dictionary definition _____

4. **gullible** : easily tricked _____

   Dictionary definition _____

5. **writhe** : squirm _____

   Dictionary definition _____

6. **pernicious** : deadly _____

   Dictionary definition _____

7. **deftly** : skillfully _____

   Dictionary definition _____

8. **copiously** : plentifully _____

   Dictionary definition _____

9. **solicitous** : considerate _____

   Dictionary definition _____

10. **steadfastly** : dependably _____

    Dictionary definition _____

Vocabulary Power *continued*

EXERCISE B Usage

If the italicized word is correct, write *correct* on the line. If not, write the correct word on the line.

1. Greg is the most *pernicious* friend I have—he'll believe anything! _____

2. As the hours wore on, the hot desert sun began to *writhe* the travelers. _____

3. After Lee had removed the blockage from the pump, the cold, clear water flowed *copiously.*

   _____

4. Racial prejudice is one of the most *solicitous* influences on young children. _____

5. I was not able to *mollify* Annie's hurt feelings about not being picked for the choir. _____

EXERCISE C Antonyms

Circle the letter of the word that is an *antonym* or opposite of the boldfaced word.

1. **solicitous**
   a. abundant   b. inconsiderate   c. caring   d. skillful

2. **poignant**
   a. bittersweet   b. attentive   c. meaningless   d. moving

3. **pernicious**
   a. firm   b. clever   c. evil   d. good

4. **mollify**
   a. irritate   b. relax   c. appease   d. twist

5. **copiously**
   a. firmly   b. easily   c. miserly   d. fully

Vocabulary Power

Lesson 3   Base Words and Word Roots

Knowing the meanings of base words and word roots can help you make an intelligent guess about the meaning of a word. Sometimes, however, the exact meaning of the new word isn't clear from the root. It's always safer to look up new words in a dictionary.

Word List

adhere	condolence	equinox	nocturnal
agnostic	doleful	inherent	prognosis
coherent	dolorous		

EXERCISE A   **Word Clues**

Read the clues. Then, write the probable definition of the boldfaced word.

1. *Dol* is a Latin root meaning "grief," "sadness," or "sorrow." Someone who is **doleful** is _____

    _____

2. *Con-* is a Latin prefix meaning "with." A **condolence** is probably _____

    _____

3. The suffix *-ous* makes a word an adjective. **Dolorous** probably means _____

    _____

4. *Haerere* is a Latin root meaning to "stick" or "cling." *Ad-* is a Latin prefix that means "to." **Adhere** probably

    means _____

5. *In-* is a Latin prefix meaning "in." **Inherent** probably means _____

    _____

6. *Co-* is a Latin prefix meaning "together." **Coherent** probably means _____

    _____

7. *Gnos, gnom* is a Greek root meaning "knowledge." *A-* is a Greek prefix that means "without" or "not."

    Someone who is an **agnostic** is _____

8. *Pro-* is a Greek prefix meaning "before" or "in front." **Prognosis** probably means _____

    _____

9. *Noct, nox* is a Latin root meaning "night." **Nocturnal** probably means _____

    _____

10. *Equi-* is a Latin prefix meaning "equal." When the **equinox** occurs, what might be happening? _____

    _____

Vocabulary Power continued

EXERCISE B Dictionary Definitions

Check your definitions by looking up each word in a dictionary. Then, write the meaning. How close did you come to the correct meaning?

1. doleful _____

2. condolence _____

3. dolorous _____

4. adhere _____

5. inherent _____

6. coherent _____

7. prognosis _____

8. agnostic _____

9. nocturnal _____

10. equinox _____

EXERCISE C Root Chart

Use a dictionary or other source to locate more words based on the roots in this lesson. List the words on the chart on this page and underline the roots. Then, quiz a partner about the meanings of the words.

dol	
haerere	
gnos, gnom	
noc, nox	

Vocabulary Power

Lesson 4   Using Reading Skills
Learning from Context: Definitions

The context of a word is the sentence or paragraph in which it appears. You can use the context to discover the meaning of an unknown word. Sometimes other words in the sentence will provide a definition.

EXERCISE A

Use context clues to find the meaning of each boldfaced word. Underline key words in the sentence that help you define the word. Then, write the word's probable meaning.

1. My uncle lived an **abstemious** life, eating and drinking in moderation.

_____

2. My brother is a dreamer who likes to just sit under a tree and **muse**, usually about life.

_____

3. In many plays, the villains often **dissemble**, hiding their real motives behind false appearances.

_____

4. The hot, humid weather robbed us of our energy and left us too **listless** even to move.

_____

5. The judge decided to **sequester** the jury so they could not possibly be influenced by TV, newspapers, or

other people. _____

6. It took only minutes for workers to **raze** the old hotel, but we still felt sad when it tumbled down.

_____

7. The neighbors' **acrimonious** argument was so loud and angry we could hear it two blocks away.

_____

8. The men who wrote the Bill of Rights believed that certain rights were **immutable** and must endure forever.

_____

9. A lack of concentration and focus now could **negate** our hard work and make it all for nothing.

_____

10. Martin spoke to the manager about the **garrulous** man who talked loudly during the whole film.

_____

EXERCISE B

Check the definition you wrote for each boldfaced word by looking it up in a dictionary. Write each definition on a separate sheet of paper; then, use each word in a sentence of your own.

Vocabulary Power

Review: Unit 1

EXERCISE

Circle the letter of the word that can best replace the word or words in italics.

1. The doctor refused to make a *prediction* about the patient's chances for recovery until he took more tests.
   a. respite   **b.** prognosis   **c.** parry   **d.** condolence

2. "I know you're uncomfortable," whispered the mother to the little girl, "but please don't *squirm* in your seat like that!"
   a. writhe   **b.** adhere   **c.** mollify   **d.** parch

3. The colonel led his troops *firmly* into battle, in spite of many dangers.
   a. deftly   **b.** steadfastly   **c.** copiously   **d.** diligently

4. "Iguana Man Emerges from Swamp" screamed the *sensational* headlines of the newspaper.
   a. gallant   **b.** lurid   **c.** furtive   **d.** pensive

5. Glorifying violence has a *deadly* effect on society.
   a. gullible   **b.** poignant   **c.** solicitous   **d.** pernicious

6. If you want to convince people of your position on an issue, your argument must be *logically consistent*.
   a. coherent   **b.** lurid   **c.** furtive   **d.** burgeoning

7. Mrs. Shapiro baked a pie for the neighbors in order to *make peace with* them after the dispute.
   a. parch   **b.** parry   **c.** mollify   **d.** writhe

8. "A penny for your thoughts," Melissa said to the *thoughtful* young man sitting next to her.
   a. pensive   **b.** gallant   **c.** pernicious   **d.** gullible

9. If we want to win the tournament, we must learn everything we can about our *opponent*.
   a. respite   **b.** prognosis   **c.** adversary   **d.** agnostic

10. After the hurricane destroyed much of the village, the air was filled with *mournful* sounds.
   a. discernable   **b.** nocturnal   **c.** furtive   **d.** dolorous

Vocabulary Power

Test: Unit 1

PART A

Circle the letter of the word that best completes the sentence.

1. We asked the company president for her _____ of economic conditions over the next two years.
   - **a.** respite
   - **b.** agnostic
   - **c.** adversary
   - **d.** prognosis

2. My tongue is going to _____ soon if I don't get a drink right now.
   - **a.** parch
   - **b.** writhe
   - **c.** adhere
   - **d.** nullify

3. Lack of efficiency is a(n) _____ weakness in the democratic governmental system.
   - **a.** coherent
   - **b.** furtive
   - **c.** inherent
   - **d.** lurid

4. Criminals sometimes trick _____ people into revealing their credit card numbers over the phone.
   - **a.** poignant
   - **b.** doleful
   - **c.** pensive
   - **d.** gullible

5. The Martins decided to go on a camping trip to celebrate the autumnal _____.
   - **a.** condolence
   - **b.** prognosis
   - **c.** equinox
   - **d.** adversary

6. The _____ interest in our school's Web site took everyone by surprise.
   - **a.** burgeoning
   - **b.** doleful
   - **c.** coherent
   - **d.** gallant

7. The _____ way the fox got into the hen house was like a story out of Aesop's fables.
   - **a.** gullible
   - **b.** furtive
   - **c.** dolorous
   - **d.** poignant

8. Before the Civil War, several Southern states tried to _____ laws passed by the U.S. government.
   - **a.** mollify
   - **b.** adhere
   - **c.** nullify
   - **d.** sequester

9. During the holidays, the cookies, cakes, and candy flowed _____ from my grandmother's kitchen.
   - **a.** copiously
   - **b.** diligently
   - **c.** steadfastly
   - **d.** deftly

10. It was difficult to make the decorations for the dance _____ to the walls without using masking tape.
    - **a.** parch
    - **b.** adhere
    - **c.** parry
    - **d.** dissemble

PART B

Circle the word in parentheses that best completes each sentence.

1. Even though the wind scattered his papers all over the lawn, Kee still delivered a (doleful, coherent, pernicious) speech.

2. The goalkeeper (deftly, copiously, diligently) plucked the soccer ball out of the air and threw it to a teammate.

3. The missionaries traveled to the village where the (pernicious, poignant, furtive) disease had taken many lives.

4. Josh worked (copiously, diligently, deftly) on his model, gluing the tiniest pieces in place with care.

5. Our family sent a card of (condolence, prognosis, respite) to the neighbors who lost their beloved dog.

Vocabulary Power continued

PART C

For each boldfaced word, circle the letter of the word that is most nearly *opposite* in meaning.

1. impulsive
   a. lurid   b. pensive   c. garrulous   d. poignant

2. indifference
   a. adversary   b. condolence   c. agnostic   d. prognosis

3. unaffecting
   a. coherent   b. immutable   c. poignant   d. abstemious

4. cowardly
   a. acrimonious   b. burgeoning   c. pensive   d. gallant

5. joyous
   a. inherent   b. nocturnal   c. doleful   d. garrulous

PART D

Circle the letter of the answer that best answers the question.

1. Which one of the following events can be described as nocturnal?
   a. a horse race   c. a fireworks display
   b. a day at the beach   d. a stroll at the park

2. Which action is a solicitous one?
   a. picking up books for someone who has dropped them   c. asking a question in class
   b. throwing snowballs at cars   d. selling candy door to door

3. Which statement would an agnostic make?
   a. "God does not exist."   c. "All religions worship the same God."
   b. "God is dead."   d. "We can't know if God exists or not."

4. How could you try to mollify someone you've had an argument with?
   a. spread rumors about the person   c. ignore the person
   b. buy the person flowers   d. play tricks on the person

5. Which news story is most likely to have a lurid headline in a newspaper?
   a. a homeless man is murdered in an alley   c. a new school is to be built
   b. the Senate debates a tax bill   d. a fire chief is to retire

Vocabulary Power

Lesson 5   Dictionary Definitions

The poets speak of love in many different ways. More than two thousand years ago, the Roman poet Virgil said love conquers all. Shakespeare claimed that love comforts like sunshine after rain. The words in this lesson will help you be able to speak about love in all its different shapes, sizes, and colors.

Word List

adamant	despondent	pertinent	scintillating
cajole	emulate	reciprocate	supplant
complacent	hamper		

EXERCISE A   Synonyms

Each boldfaced word is paired with a synonym whose meaning you probably know. For each pair, think of other related words. Then, look up the word in a dictionary and write its meaning.

1. **despondent** : depressed _____

   Dictionary definition _____

2. **reciprocate** : return _____

   Dictionary definition _____

3. **supplant** : replace _____

   Dictionary definition _____

4. **scintillating** : sparkling _____

   Dictionary definition _____

5. **pertinent** : relevant _____

   Dictionary definition _____

6. **complacent** : self-satisfied _____

   Dictionary definition _____

7. **cajole** : coax _____

   Dictionary definition _____

8. **hamper** : restrain _____

   Dictionary definition _____

9. **adamant** : inflexible _____

   Dictionary definition _____

10. **emulate** : imitate _____

    Dictionary definition _____

Vocabulary Power continued

EXERCISE B Word Meanings

Answer each question.

1. Give one rule for personal behavior you feel **adamant** about. _____
_____

2. Who is someone you try to **emulate**? Why? _____
_____

3. Explain how not getting enough sleep can **hamper** earning good grades. _____
_____

4. What would you say to a good friend who was feeling **despondent**? _____
_____

5. Who do you think has the most **scintillating** personality in your school? Give an example of this person's
scintillating behavior. _____
_____

EXERCISE C Usage

Write the word that best completes the sentence.

1. Oswald refused to put his age on the job application because it was not _____
information.

2. The team lost in the playoffs because their undefeated record made the players feel _____
about their opponents.

3. Bekka's little sister tried to _____ Bekka into going to the theme park.

4. After defeating Robert in the tournament, Tia was able to _____ Robert as the top player
in the chess club.

5. In many cultures, when you receive a gift, you are expected to _____ with another gift.

6. The doctor was feeling _____ over her inability to help her cancer patients.

7. Will your sprained ankle _____ your efforts to make the volleyball team?

Vocabulary Power

Lesson 6 Word Families

A word family is made up of words that have a common origin or root. The root or base word gives a word its main meaning. Adding a prefix or suffix to the word root gives it a different meaning. In this lesson, you'll learn the Greek root *dem* and the Latin roots *dur* and *pen*.

Word List

demagogue	endemic	obdurate	penance
demographic	endurance	pandemic	penitent
duress	epidemic		

EXERCISE A Dictionary Definitions

Look up each boldfaced word in a dictionary and write its meaning. Then, use the information in the dictionary to underline the root or base word.

1. obdurate _____

2. duress _____

3. endurance _____

4. penance _____

5. penitent _____

6. endemic _____

7. demographic _____

8. demagogue _____

9. pandemic _____

10. epidemic _____

EXERCISE B Root Meanings

Write the main meaning of the word roots in this lesson.

1. *dur* _____

_____

2. *pen* _____

_____

3. *dem* _____

_____

Vocabulary Power *continued*

EXERCISE C Word Webs

Use the word webs below to note other words from the word families in this lesson. For each word web, add as many other words as you can that contain the same root. Underline the root in each new word. You may use a dictionary to find words in the word families.

dur

pen

dem

EXERCISE D Composing Sentences

On a separate sheet of paper, write a sentence of your own for each vocabulary word.

Vocabulary Power

Vocabulary Power

Lesson 7   Connotation and Denotation

A word's *denotation* is its dictionary meaning. Its *connotation* is the feelings and ideas associated with the word. It's important to know a word's connotation. For example, if you were writing about a flower, you might choose the word *fragrance,* since the word is associated with pleasant smells. However, if you were writing about a barnyard or garbage dump, you might choose the word *odor.* Most people associate this word with unpleasant smells. Some words, like *smell,* are neutral. Both flowers and barnyards smell. In this lesson, you'll learn about the connotations and denotations of words.

Word List

lavish	notoriety	smirk	unkempt
methodical	paltry	torpor	venture
mundane	reproach		

EXERCISE A   Word Meanings

On the chart below, write several synonyms for each of the following boldfaced words. Write a plus beside the synonym if you feel it has a positive connotation. Write a minus beside it if you feel it has a negative connotation. If you feel the word is neutral, with neither a positive nor a negative connotation, place an *X* beside it.

lavish	
methodical	
venture	
unkempt	
torpor	
smirk	
reproach	
paltry	
mundane	
notoriety	

Vocabulary Power *continued*

EXERCISE B Word Meanings
Circle the letter of the sentence that best expresses the connotative meaning of each boldfaced word.

1. lavish
   a. The main ballroom of the Crystal Palace is lavish in its decor.
   b. Lavish rain swept the mountainside.

2. methodical
   a. The commander ordered his troops to line up in methodical rows.
   b. The housekeeper did her daily tasks in a methodical way.

3. venture
   a. The worker decided to venture over to the food cart to get a sandwich.
   b. The financier chose to venture most of his capital on the bull market.

4. unkempt
   a. Blown by the strong wind, her unkempt hair stuck up in all directions.
   b. The teacher rejected the unkempt paper because of coffee stains.

5. torpor
   a. Most human beings experience a state of torpor at bedtime.
   b. Hibernating animals spend the winter in a state of torpor.

6. smirk
   a. The thief could not conceal a smirk when he heard the "Not Guilty" verdict.
   b. The little girl had a sweet smirk on her face as she rode the pony.

7. reproach
   a. The mother reproached her three-year-old for crying.
   b. After the robbery, Mr. Jones reproached himself for leaving the door unlocked.

8. paltry
   a. Human beings are becoming more aware that their differences are paltry.
   b. After touring the royal palace, the college student thought her dorm room looked paltry.

9. mundane
   a. Activities such as paying bills and doing laundry are mundane but necessary.
   b. Johnnie spent his allowance on a mundane purchase, a new car.

10. notoriety
    a. The con artist's notoriety preceded him everywhere he went.
    b. The writer's notoriety was based on his talent.

EXERCISE C Multiple-Meaning Words
The words *lavish* and *venture* have more than one meaning. On a separate piece of paper, write two sentences for each word that demonstrate two of its different meanings. After each sentence, write the definition you used.

Name _____ Date _____ Class _____

Vocabulary Power

Lesson 8   Using Reference Skills
Using a Dictionary: Word Origins
Many English words have their origins in other languages. In a dictionary, the origin of a word is usually given in brackets at the beginning or end of the definition. Here is a sample dictionary entry.

> **hypocrisy** *n.* (hi pä' kra sē) pretending to be what one is not, or to believe what one does not; the false assumption of an appearance of virtue or religion [from Greek *hypokrinesthai,* to play a part on the stage, answer]

EXERCISE
Use a dictionary to answer each question.

1. What is the definition and origin of the word **saunter?** _____
   _____

   Why might someone who is sauntering also be likely to **muse?** _____
   _____

2. What is the difference in the meanings of the words **egregious** and **gregarious?** _____
   _____

   What agricultural word root are these two words based on? _____
   _____

3. How does a **stoic** respond to life's events? _____
   _____

   What is this word's connection with porches? _____
   _____

4. If you received a **tawdry** gift, would you be pleased? Why or why not? _____
   _____

   What is this word's connection to lace? _____
   _____

5. If something happened to **kindle** your interest in a subject, what would be your likely next step? _____
   _____

   What is this word's origin? _____

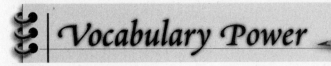

Vocabulary Power

Review: Unit 2

EXERCISE A

Circle the word in parentheses that best completes the sentence.

1. Rita had been lying in the hot sun so long that nothing could disturb her (endurance, torpor, notoriety).

2. "I'm afraid we may be looking at a serious typhoid (epidemic, pandemic, venture)," said the doctor.

3. The advertising campaign for soda was directed at a specific (mundane, penitent, demographic) segment.

4. The host invited many celebrities so that the New Year's Eve party would be a (mundane, pertinent, scintillating) event.

5. The new business (venture, duress, demagogue) proved to be a loss for its investors.

6. Troy wanted to wear his lizardskin cowboy boots under his graduation gown, but his mother was (penitent, adamant, unkempt) in her opposition.

7. Don't you find it hard to do favors for people who never (reciprocate, lavish, hamper) your kindness?

8. I admired the (endemic, complacent, methodical) way Elena separated each small strand of hair before she braided them.

9. By trying to create a pure German nation, Adolf Hitler became the best-known (epidemic, venture, demagogue) of this century.

10. Jesse James's (torpor, notoriety, endurance) is known to anyone who has read about the Wild West.

EXERCISE B

Circle the letter of the word that is a synonym for the word or phrase listed.

1. criticize
   a. reproach   **b.** smirk   **c.** cajole   **d.** hamper

2. stubborn
   a. obdurate   **b.** pandemic   **c.** mundane   **d.** adamant

3. take the place of
   a. reproach   **b.** supplant   **c.** lavish   **d.** reciprocate

4. sloppy
   a. mundane   **b.** obdurate   **c.** despondent   **d.** unkempt

5. despairing
   a. despondent   **b.** lavish   **c.** paltry   **d.** pertinent

Vocabulary Power

Test: Unit 2

PART A

Circle the letter of the word that best completes each sentence.

1. Kayla would _____ at everyone's suggestions for the party, but she didn't contribute any ideas of her own.
   a. cajole   **b.** smirk   **c.** reciprocate   **d.** supplant

2. Some people probably find working in the garden _____, but I think it's exciting to watch things grow.
   a. complacent   **b.** despondent   **c.** mundane   **d.** scintillating

3. The bride-to-be hoped her friends would not _____ her with gifts at her second shower.
   a. supplant   **b.** emulate   **c.** lavish   **d.** reciprocate

4. Worry about the economic future became _____ among the townspeople when the factory closed.
   a. pandemic   **b.** epidemic   **c.** endemic   **d.** complacent

5. The king was required by the church to do _____ for his evil deeds.
   a. penance   **b.** torpor   **c.** endurance   **d.** duress

6. The cactus is not _____ in my home state of Maine, although it is in Arizona.
   a. penitent   **b.** unkempt   **c.** endemic   **d.** obdurate

7. Your _____ will be tested if you run in the marathon next month.
   a. venture   **b.** endurance   **c.** notoriety   **d.** penance

8. Lily feared that her lack of geometry would _____ her attempt to become an engineer.
   a. hamper   **b.** emulate   **c.** supplant   **d.** reproach

9. Even though she expected to win, the candidate did not become _____ and continued to campaign.
   a. penitent   **b.** obdurate   **c.** complacent   **d.** methodical

10. You can plead, nag, and _____ all you want, but I will not sell you my tuba!
    a. hamper   **b.** smirk   **c.** lavish   **d.** cajole

11. Building a model of the Taj Mahal out of toothpicks certainly takes a _____ worker.
    a. penitent   **b.** methodical   **c.** mundane   **d.** despondent

12. The researchers planned a(n) _____ study to find out who would be most likely to buy the skates.
    a. scintillating   **b.** despondent   **c.** demographic   **d.** unkempt

13. No parents could be more _____ than mine about not watching television until my homework is finished.
    a. adamant   **b.** despondent   **c.** pertinent   **d.** penitent

14. The bank robber's _____ made it easy for the police to recognize him at the airport.
    a. notoriety   **b.** endurance   **c.** penance   **d.** venture

Vocabulary Power continued

15. The Rangers hoped to _____ the Yankees as World Series champions.

    a. cajole   **b.** reciprocate   **c.** reproach   **d.** supplant

16. Although dogs aren't evil, Max's need to chase cars seems almost _____.

    a. obdurate   **b.** complacent   **c.** demographic   **d.** mundane

17. When the buyers offered the _____ sum of ten dollars, David almost laughed at how low it was.

    a. pertinent   **b.** paltry   **c.** adamant   **d.** unkempt

18. You can borrow my CD player if you're willing to _____ when I need to borrow something.

    a. supplant   **b.** emulate   **c.** hamper   **d.** reciprocate

19. The teachers nervously discussed the near-_____ of failing grades in the senior class.

    a. venture   **b.** torpor   **c.** epidemic   **d.** notoriety

20. The lizard's _____, under the hot desert sun, made the lizard easy prey for the hawk.

    a. duress   **b.** torpor   **c.** endurance   **d.** penance

PART B

Circle the letter of the word that is most nearly *opposite* in meaning of the boldfaced word.

1. despondent

    a. depressed   **b.** bored   **c.** cheerful   **d.** indifferent

2. duress

    a. stress   **b.** ease   **c.** hardiness   **d.** stimulation

3. scintillating

    a. exciting   **b.** sinful   **c.** shining   **d.** dull

4. unkempt

    a. free   **b.** concerned   **c.** neat   **d.** messy

5. penitent

    a. unashamed   **b.** healthy   **c.** sorrowful   **d.** happy

Vocabulary Power

Lesson 9   Using Synonyms

Have you read Shakespeare's play *Macbeth*? It tells the story of a talented and brave Scottish noble whose ambition leads him to commit a dreadful murder and seize the royal throne—with tragic consequences for everyone. The words in this lesson can help you examine ambition, along with the anguish that sometimes accompanies it.

Word List

avarice	depravity	obstreperous	quandary
blighted	fecund	predominance	surfeited
constraint	megalomania		

EXERCISE A   Synonyms

Each boldfaced vocabulary word below is paired with a synonym whose meaning you probably know. Think of other words related to the synonym and write your ideas. Then, look up the word in a dictionary and write its meaning.

1. **predominance** : holding the most power _____

   Dictionary definition _____

2. **constraint** : restriction _____

   Dictionary definition _____

3. **obstreperous** : loudly defiant _____

   Dictionary definition _____

4. **surfeited** : overfed _____

   Dictionary definition _____

5. **depravity** : corruption _____

   Dictionary definition _____

6. **quandary** : predicament _____

   Dictionary definition _____

7. **avarice** : greed _____

   Dictionary definition _____

8. **fecund** : fertile _____

   Dictionary definition _____

9. **blighted** : ruined _____

   Dictionary definition _____

10. **megalomania** : insane fantasy of power _____

    Dictionary definition _____

Vocabulary Power *continued*

EXERCISE B Usage
Answer each question.

1. Why do you think some people develop extreme **avarice?** _____

_____

_____

2. Describe a **quandary** in which you recently found yourself. _____

_____

_____

3. How would you deal with an **obstreperous** customer at a store where you work? _____

_____

_____

4. Do you believe the government should place any kind of **constraint** on the right of Americans to own

guns? Why or why not? _____

_____

_____

5. What might explain the **predominance** of comedy shows on prime-time television? _____

_____

_____

6. What is one way that society could deal with **blighted** city neighborhoods? _____

_____

_____

7. What is one example of something involved in a **surfeited** lifestyle? _____

_____

_____

8. What people would you least expect **depravity** from? _____

_____

_____

9. How would you expect a person with **megalomania** to act? _____

_____

_____

10. Would a **fecund** tomato be something you'd want? Why or why not? _____

_____

_____

Vocabulary Power

Lesson 10   Word Roots *terr, lun,* and *astr*

The Latin root *terr* means "earth." The Latin root *lun* means "moon." The Greek root *astr* means "star." All the vocabulary words in this lesson have one of these roots as their root part. The root part of a word carries the word's main meaning. In most of these words, a prefix (at the beginning) or suffix (at the end) has been added to the root word to modify its meaning.

Word List

astral	lunacy	terrace	terrestrial
astronomer	lunatic	terrarium	territorial
inter	sublunary		

EXERCISE A   Roots

Underline the root part of each boldfaced vocabulary word. Then, look up the word in a dictionary and write its meaning.

1. territorial _____

2. terrarium _____

3. inter _____

4. terrace _____

5. terrestrial _____

6. lunacy _____

7. sublunary _____

8. lunatic _____

9. astral _____

10. astronomer _____

EXERCISE B   Usage

Answer each question based on your understanding of the boldfaced vocabulary word.

1. What advantages does a **terrace** have over a porch? What are some disadvantages? _____
_____

2. How would you answer someone who argued that it is **lunacy** to allow sixteen-year-olds to drive cars?
_____

3. What kinds of plants and animals might you want to place in a **terrarium?** _____
_____

Vocabulary Power *continued*

4. Would it interest you to become an **astronomer**? Why or why not? _____

_____

5. Do you believe that anyone who commits a terrorist act is a **lunatic**? Explain your answer. _____

_____

EXERCISE C **Sentence Construction**

Write a sentence of your own using each boldfaced word.

1. territorial _____

2. sublunary _____

3. terrestrial _____

4. inter _____

5. astral _____

EXERCISE D **Movie Summaries**

Here are the titles of three new movies. Use your imagination—and a vocabulary word from this lesson—to write a short summary of each movie.

1. *Monkeys in Space, Part 2: Bobo's Revenge* _____

_____

_____

_____

2. *It Attacked from Beyond the Grave* _____

_____

_____

_____

3. *A Mind Is a Terrible Thing to Lose* _____

_____

_____

_____

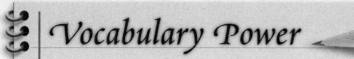
Vocabulary Power

Lesson 11   Prefixes That Show Negation

Knowing the meaning of prefixes can help you discover the meanings of unknown words. A large number of prefixes show negation. These can mean *not, against, bad* or *badly, the opposite of, wrong, failure,* or *lack of.* Some of these prefixes are *non-, ir-, a-, mal-, anti-, de-, dis-, ob-, op-,* and *il-.* Be careful, though. Not all words that begin with these letter combinations have the meaning of the prefix. When in doubt, look up the word in a dictionary.

Word List

amoral	disconsolate	malcontent	oblivious
antipathy	illusory	nonentity	opprobrium
derogatory	irrelevant		

EXERCISE A **Prefixes**

Underline the prefix in each boldfaced vocabulary word. Answer the question on the basis of the clues. Then, check the definition of the vocabulary word in a dictionary and write its meaning.

1. **nonentity** : The word *entity* means "something that exists" and is a form of the Latin verb *esse,* "to be."

   The word **nonentity** probably means _____

   Dictionary definition _____

2. **irrelevant** : Something that is relevant has some connection with the matter at hand. If an argument is

   irrelevant, what connection does it have to the matter at hand? _____

   Dictionary definition _____

3. **amoral** : Someone with good values is *moral,* while someone with evil values in *immoral.* How might you

   describe someone who is **amoral**? _____

   Dictionary definition _____

4. **malcontent** : A contented person is one who is satisfied with things as they are. How would a **malcontent**

   feel about the existing system? _____

   Dictionary definition _____

5. **antipathy** : Pathos is an emotion of pity. Sympathy is sharing emotion with someone. But if you have

   antipathy toward someone, what kind of feeling would you have? _____

   Dictionary definition _____

6. **derogatory** : *Roga* is a Latin root meaning "to ask." When a negation prefix is attached to this root, the

   result is a word that probably means _____

   Dictionary definition _____

Vocabulary Power continued

7. disconsolate : To console someone is to offer your sympathy or comfort. How would you guess someone

who is **disconsolate** feels? _____

Dictionary definition _____

8. oblivious : The Latin root *liv* means "to wipe," and the negation prefix *ob-* can mean "away." If you are

oblivious to something, what is your relation to it? _____

Dictionary definition _____

9. illusory : The original meaning of the Latin word on which *illusory* is based is "to mock," or literally

"to play against" something. If something is **illusory**, can you trust that it is what it appears to be? Why or

why not?

_____

Dictionary definition _____

10. opprobrium : The Latin word *probum* means "criticism." Adding the negation prefix *op-* creates a word

that probably means _____

Dictionary definition _____

EXERCISE B Usage

Answer each question based on your understanding of the boldfaced vocabulary word.

1. How would you respond to someone's claim that the progress of society over the last century is **illusory**?

_____

2. Imagine that you want to get a dog but that your mother has an **antipathy** toward pets. How would you go

about trying to change her mind? _____

_____

3. Why, do you think, is it easier for some people to make **derogatory** comments than pleasant remarks?

_____

4. What techniques do you use to remain **oblivious** to surrounding noises when you are trying to study?

_____

5. Do you believe that gender is **irrelevant** to job performance? Explain your answer. _____

_____

EXERCISE C Words in Print

**Words that begin with negation prefixes appear often in newspapers and magazines. On a
separate sheet of paper, make a list of words you find containing these prefixes. After each word,
use context or a dictionary to write a definition of the word.**

Vocabulary Power

Lesson 12   Using Reading Skills
Learning from Context

The *context* of a word is the environment in which it appears. You can use the context to discover the meaning of an unknown vocabulary word. Look for key words elsewhere in the sentence that will help you define the unknown word. Sometimes other words in the sentence will provide examples that will help you discover the definition of the unknown word.

EXERCISE

Read each sentence. Use the context to find the meaning of the boldfaced word. On the first line, jot down the examples in the sentence that help you define the unknown vocabulary word. Then, write the probable meaning of the boldfaced word on the second line.

1. During the Revolutionary War, the British made use of **mercenary** soldiers, such as the Hessians, who were paid to fight the American rebels. _____

_____

2. The speaker's **pithy** comment, "What goes around, comes around," struck everyone in the audience as extremely appropriate to the occasion. _____

_____

3. The **quagmire** at La Brea in Los Angeles contains the preserved bones of prehistoric creatures like the woolly mammoth. _____

_____

4. If you really want to impress someone, walk around with a weighty **tome** like *Moby-Dick, The Scarlet Letter,* or *David Copperfield* under your arm. _____

_____

5. I consider Thomas Jefferson the most **urbane** of American presidents, but my friend says Abraham Lincoln tops her list. _____

_____

6. The mosquitoes, flies, barking dogs, loud radio, snoring from the next tent, and the endless drizzle all combined to **vex** me during the camping trip. _____

_____

7. Please **apprise** me of your decision by fax, phone, letter, or e-mail as quickly as you can._____

_____

8. Phoning at two o'clock in the morning, walking in without knocking, eating out of our refrigerator, and calling my great-grandmother "Babe"—all these have made me realize that Joshua is a real **boor.**

_____

Vocabulary Power

Review: Unit 3

EXERCISE

Circle the word in parentheses that best completes the sentence.

1. The relatives decided to wait until Tuesday to (vex, inter, deviate) the accident victim.

2. The spacecraft's (amoral, terrestrial, astral) journey was estimated to take about ninety years.

3. My little brother was absolutely (disconsolate, pithy, surfeited) about losing his new Swiss army knife on the campout.

4. To many people, the legend of King Midas and his golden touch is a powerful reminder of the dangers of (constraint, avarice, antipathy).

5. The soybean fields looked (disconsolate, blighted, oblivious) because of the plague of grasshoppers.

6. The headwaiter at the fancy restaurant was forced to call the police to remove the (urbane, illusory, obstreperous) customer.

7. The rich soil on my uncle's farm in western Ohio is among the most (fecund, blighted, derogatory) in the country.

8. Michelle will be hard to work with on the project unless she is able to overcome her (depravity, derogatory, antipathy) for getting her hands dirty.

9. Paying that much money for such a tiny apartment is complete (lunacy, quandary, antipathy)!

10. I realize that I'm not on the student council, but that's no reason for her to treat me like a (tome, nonentity, astronomer).

Vocabulary Power

Test: Unit 3

PART A

Circle the letter of the word that best completes the sentence.

1. Raising the fines for speeding seems to place no _____ on those drivers who continue to race past the elementary school.
   a. antipathy   **b.** opprobrium   **c.** constraint   **d.** megalomania

2. Our society must find a way to deal with the _____ before he or she inflicts violence on others.
   a. malcontent   **b.** terrace   **c.** astronomer   **d.** quagmire

3. When Stephen did not see his name on the cast list, he realized that his hopes for landing a role had been _____.
   a. illusory   **b.** irrelevant   **c.** derogatory   **d.** pithy

4. Only a(n) _____ would try to fly off the barn roof using wings made of plastic straws and chicken feathers!
   a. astronomer   **b.** malcontent   **c.** lunatic   **d.** boor

5. The dictator's _____ knew no limits; soon his illegal seizure of power aroused global criticism.
   a. opprobrium   **b.** constraint   **c.** megalomania   **d.** predominance

6. The meal of pop, doughnuts, brownies, ice cream, and candy left Jeffrey feeling more than a little _____ with sugar.
   a. surfeited   **b.** disconsolate   **c.** derogatory   **d.** blighted

7. The _____ of girls over boys in the advanced mathematics class represented a major change from the preceding decade.
   a. quandary   **b.** predominance   **c.** antipathy   **d.** depravity

8. "How I long for true excitement," sighed Rose, "but I fear my life will continue in its dreadfully boring pattern in this dull, _____ world."
   a. fecund   **b.** astral   **c.** sublunary   **d.** urbane

9. The committee members are tired of hearing purely _____ remarks that do not offer any positive suggestions.
   a. territorial   **b.** amoral   **c.** derogatory   **d.** sublunary

10. My dog found himself in a _____: should he chase the neighbor's cat or should he eat the juicy hot dog that fell off the grill?
   a. terrace   **b.** quandary   **c.** nonentity   **d.** megalomania

Vocabulary Power *continued*

PART B

Circle the letter of the word that best answers the question.

1. If someone has no interest in basketball, how would he probably feel if the school team advanced to the district finals?

   a. disconsolate   **b.** obstreperous   **c.** oblivious   **d.** amoral

2. Which would you be most likely to find attached to the rear of your house?

   a. terrarium   **b.** terrace   **c.** terrestrial   **d.** quagmire

3. To what type of person are the terms "right" and "wrong" meaningless?

   a. disconsolate   **b.** amoral   **c.** surfeited   **d.** pithy

4. What characteristic would a miser be showing if he sits all day in a bank vault playing with his stacks of money?

   a. irrelevant   **b.** avarice   **c.** constraint   **d.** antipathy

5. Whom would you consult if you wanted information on the solar system?

   a. a lunatic   **b.** a malcontent   **c.** an astronomer   **d.** a nonentity

6. Which word describes a giraffe, but not a dolphin?

   a. terrestrial   **b.** obstreperous   **c.** irrelevant   **d.** disconsolate

7. If a senator votes for a tax increase while the people she represents are strongly opposed to any tax hikes, which would she probably receive?

   a. avarice   **b.** predominance   **c.** opprobrium   **d.** terrarium

8. If you were a server in a restaurant, which kind of customer would you *least* like to serve?

   a. an obstreperous one   **c.** a surfeited one
   b. a sublunary one   **d.** a territorial one

9. If Shania is going to plant a vegetable garden, what kind of soil is likely to give her the best yield?

   a. blighted soil   **b.** terrestrial soil   **c.** fecund soil   **d.** illusory soil

10. What is a soldier-for-hire called?

   a. a terrace   **b.** a mercenary   **c.** a tome   **d.** a terrarium

Name _____ Date _____ Class _____

Vocabulary Power

Lesson 13   Word Usage

Inspiration comes in many forms. The sound of music, a clear blue sky, a thoughtful speech—all of these things can uplift and energize us. Inspiration often comes unexpectedly, like a gift. But you can also deliberately seek and find inspiration by exposing yourself to new ideas, people, and experiences. The words in this list relate to the theme of inspirations.

> **Word List**
>
> | | | | |
> |---|---|---|---|
> | adroit | grandiose | opportune | subterranean |
> | enmity | inept | outlandish | whimsical |
> | frivolous | ingenious | | |

EXERCISE A   Synonyms

Each boldfaced vocabulary word is paired with a synonym whose meaning you probably know. Think of other words related to the synonym and write your ideas. Then, look up the vocabulary word in a dictionary and write its meaning.

1. **opportune** : timely _____

   Dictionary definition _____

2. **grandiose** : grand _____

   Dictionary definition _____

3. **whimsical** : playful _____

   Dictionary definition _____

4. **ingenious** : inventive _____

   Dictionary definition _____

5. **outlandish** : strange _____

   Dictionary definition _____

6. **subterranean** : underground _____

   Dictionary definition _____

7. **enmity** : hatred _____

   Dictionary definition _____

8. **frivolous** : silly _____

   Dictionary definition _____

9. **inept** : clumsy _____

   Dictionary definition _____

10. **adroit** : skillful _____

    Dictionary definition _____

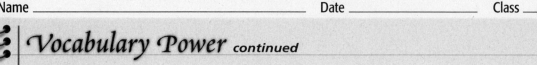

Vocabulary Power *continued*

EXERCISE B Usage

If the boldfaced word is used correctly in the sentence, write correct above it. If not, draw a line through the word and write the correct vocabulary word above it.

1. The police officer passed by at an **opportune** moment because someone had just stolen my backpack.

2. The **frivolous** house featured sixteen bedrooms, a ballroom, and Italian marble floors in the entry.

3. Instead of feeling **enmity** for one's persecutors, the pastor urged patience and understanding.

4. The politician, an **adroit** campaigner, moved through the crowd, making brief remarks, shaking hands, and kissing babies.

5. Marcellus came up with the **outlandish** idea of starting a recycling program in his district.

6. The comedian is known for his **grandiose** stunts; he once delivered his entire monologue standing on his head.

7. Claire took a **subterranean** vacation; she explored several underground caves in Kentucky.

8. The **whimsical** badminton player apologized for colliding frequently with his partner.

9. **Ingenious** details are not important when you are being questioned by a lawyer in a court of law.

10. That gift shop sells many **inept** items; I once purchased an inflatable pickle there.

EXERCISE C Sentence Completion

Write the vocabulary word that best completes each sentence.

1. Glen feels _____ at playing soccer because he doesn't know the rules.

2. This version of *The Nutcracker* is very happy and _____.

3. They performed the play on a(n) _____ and extravagant scale.

4. She had a very _____ way of spending money on her frequent shopping trips.

5. Anita was very _____ at producing her work efficiently.

6. At an awkward pause in the conversation, there was a(n) _____ knock at the door.

7. Our class created a wonderfully _____ contraption for walking a dog.

8. We had a class trip to the nearby _____ caves where millions of bats live.

9. Sandy is very proud to show her _____ clothes.

10. There is a great _____ between those brothers–they fight all the time!

Vocabulary Power

Lesson 14   Suffixes That Form Nouns

A suffix is a word ending that can be added to a word or root. Adding a suffix modifies the meaning of the word and also changes the word's part of speech. For example, the suffixes -ty (-ity) and -ation both mean "state, condition, or quality." Adding these suffixes changes the form of the word to a noun. For example the word *sincerity (sincere + ity)* means "the quality of being sincere" and *preservation (preserve + ation)* means "the state of being preserved."

Word List

laceration	obfuscation	procrastination	propensity
legibility	paucity	proliferation	viability
levitation	piety		

EXERCISE A   Usage

Use the meaning of the suffix and the information given about the base word or root to come up with a possible meaning for each word. Then, look up the word in a dictionary and write its definition.

1. *Pious* means "religious." **Piety** might mean _____

   Dictionary definition _____

2. *Legible* means "readable." **Legibility** might mean _____

   Dictionary definition _____

3. *Viable* means "capable of life" or "success." **Viability** might mean _____

   Dictionary definition _____

4. The root *pauc* means "little" or "few." **Paucity** might mean _____

   Dictionary definition _____

5. The root *propend* means "to lean." **Propensity** might mean _____

   Dictionary definition _____

6. *Procrastinate* means "to delay." **Procrastination** might mean _____

   Dictionary definition _____

7. *Proliferate* means "to multiply." **Proliferation** might mean _____

   Dictionary definition _____

8. *Levitate* means "to rise" or "float in the air." **Levitation** might mean _____

   Dictionary definition _____

9. *Lacerate* means "to tear roughly." **Laceration** might mean _____

   Dictionary definition _____

10. *Obfuscate* means "to confuse." **Obfuscation** might mean _____

   Dictionary definition _____

Vocabulary Power *continued*

EXERCISE B Sentence Completion
Write the vocabulary word that correctly completes each sentence.

1. When food was rationed during the war, there was a(n) _____ of luxuries such as sugar and coffee.

2. The audience was startled when the singer rose into the air, but I could see that this false _____ was accomplished using well-concealed ropes.

3. The _____ of mice in the barn is due to the fact that we gave our cat away.

4. The jagged wound on the soldier's leg was a(n) _____ caused by barbed wire.

5. Because both of the speakers had engaged in _____, we left the debate still confused about the issues.

6. Isaiah has a(n) _____ for interrupting others; I've noticed this both in class and in casual conversation.

7. "The _____ of your homework is very poor, " said the teacher.

8. It is difficult to avoid _____ and actually work over the holidays.

EXERCISE C Clues Matching
Write the vocabulary word that fits each clue.

1. Nuns have plenty of this.   _____

2. A plan that falls flat would not have this.   _____

3. The handwriting of many teachers has this quality.   _____

4. Some students behind in their school work have this habit.   _____

5. You could get one of these playing by broken glass.   _____

6. An explanation by a parent that confuses you.   _____

7. A magician floating an assistant over the audience.   _____

8. When there is an overabundance of books in a library.   _____

Vocabulary Power

Lesson 15   Prefixes That Show Direction or Position

A prefix is a word part attached at the beginning of a base word or root. Listed below are several prefixes that show direction or position. Knowing the meaning of these prefixes can help you figure out the meaning of unfamiliar words.

Prefix	Meaning	Example	Definition
extra-	outside, to the outside	extracurricular	outside the curriculum
inter-	between	interrupt	stop by breaking in between
sub-	under, beneath, below	subclass	group below a class
super-	over, above	superhuman	exceeding normal human power
trans-	across, beyond, through	transfer	move or carry to a different place

Word List

extrapolate	intersperse	superficial	transcend
extravagant	subjugate	superfluous	transgress
intermediary	subservient		

EXERCISE A Prefixes

For each word, underline the prefix and list another word you know that contains the prefix. Then, look up the vocabulary word in a dictionary and write its definition.

1. extravagant _____

   Dictionary definition _____

2. intermediary _____

   Dictionary definition _____

3. subjugate _____

   Dictionary definition _____

4. superficial _____

   Dictionary definition _____

5. transcend _____

   Dictionary definition _____

6. extrapolate _____

   Dictionary definition _____

7. intersperse _____

   Dictionary definition _____

♪ Vocabulary Power continued

8. subservient _____

Dictionary definition _____

9. superfluous _____

Dictionary definition _____

10. transgress _____

Dictionary definition _____

EXERCISE B Usage

Circle the vocabulary word in parentheses that best completes each sentence.

1. A power-hungry emperor might (transcend, subjugate, extrapolate) the people of a neighboring country.

2. Using data gathered through a public opinion poll, you could (intersperse, extrapolate, transgress) the probable election results.

3. A person with a(n) (subservient, superfluous, extravagant) attitude might agree to every suggestion you make without question or complaint.

4. If your analysis of a novel lacked depth, a critic might say it was (superfluous, superficial, subservient).

5. If you gave someone (superficial, extravagant, superfluous) compliments, they might feel embarrassed by the excess of your remarks.

EXERCISE C Sentence Completion

Write the vocabulary word that best completes each sentence.

1. The agent for the well-known actor served as a(n) _____ in negotiating film contracts with movie producers.

2. Calvin planned to _____ clumps of daffodils among the dark green myrtle that served as ground cover.

3. There are serious penalties if you _____ the criminal laws of this state.

4. As Reggie edited his letter to the newspaper, he deleted _____ words to shorten the letter and strengthen his argument.

5. Both movies _____ the science fiction category; they have universal themes and sympathetic and dignified characters.

Vocabulary Power

Lesson 16   Using Reference Skills
Using a Thesaurus: Synonyms and Antonyms

A thesaurus, a reference tool that lists synonyms, can help you pinpoint the particular word you need in writing. Many thesauruses are in dictionary form; that is, the entries are listed alphabetically, as in the sample below. Synonyms with a common basic meaning are grouped together. In some cases, antonyms, words with the opposite meaning, are also given. Entries for more specific words usually include a cross-reference to a general word with the same basic meaning. If you turn to that entry, you can find a larger selection of related words.

> **lenient** *adj.* – *Syn.* loving, soft, soft-hearted, mild, yielding, pampering, indulgent, tolerant; see also **kind.** – *Ant.* severe, firm, austere.
> **leverage** *n.* – *Syn.* purchase, lift, hold; see **support 2.**
> **liable** *adj.* **1.** [Responsible] – *Syn.* answerable, subject, accountable; see **responsible 1.   2.** [Likely] – *Syn.* verisimilar, apt, inclined; see **likely 5.**
> **liberal** *n.* **1.** [Open-handed] – *Syn.* unselfish, bountiful, benevolent; see **generous 1, kind.   2.** [Open-minded] tolerant, receptive, progressive, advanced, left, radical, broad-minded, permissive, left-wing; see also **fair 1.**

EXERCISE

Use the sample thesaurus entries above to answer the questions about synonyms and antonyms.

1. What is one synonym for the word **lenient?** _____ What is one word that has the opposite meaning of this word? _____

2. Under what general entry should you look to find additional words that share the meaning of the word **leverage?** _____ What specific subentry for that word should you check?_____
   _____

3. What are the two basic meanings of the word **liable?** _____

4. If you were writing a paper about a presidential election, which synonyms for **liberal** might you use?
   _____

5. If you were having trouble deciding whether to use **severe** or **austere** as an antonym for **lenient,** how could you find out exactly how the two words differ in meaning? _____
   _____

6. Substitute an appropriate synonym for the boldfaced word in each phrase:

   Liberal quantities of ice cream _____

   Liberal in lending equipment _____

Vocabulary Power

Review: Unit 4

EXERCISE

Circle the letter of the word that best matches each clue.

1. a plan to transform the U.S. highway system
   - **a.** grandiose
   - **b.** frivolous
   - **c.** inept
   - **d.** intermediary

2. wearing a large fish as a hat
   - **a.** superfluous
   - **b.** superficial
   - **c.** opportune
   - **d.** outlandish

3. the reason a term paper is not completed by the deadline
   - **a.** procrastination
   - **b.** proliferation
   - **c.** levitation
   - **d.** obfuscation

4. a tiny scratch on the skin
   - **a.** extravagant
   - **b.** outlandish
   - **c.** superficial
   - **d.** intermediary

5. a birthday gift of $1000
   - **a.** superficial
   - **b.** whimsical
   - **c.** adroit
   - **d.** extravagant

6. a car that runs on water instead of gasoline
   - **a.** levitation
   - **b.** ingenious
   - **c.** subterranean
   - **d.** inept

7. someone who is always dropping and breaking things
   - **a.** grandiose
   - **b.** opportune
   - **c.** inept
   - **d.** adroit

8. extremely bad feelings between individuals
   - **a.** paucity
   - **b.** enmity
   - **c.** obfuscation
   - **d.** propensity

9. location of the subway
   - **a.** subterranean
   - **b.** frivolous
   - **c.** whimsical
   - **d.** outlandish

10. someone with the ability to handle a problem with skill
    - **a.** inept
    - **b.** adroit
    - **c.** opportune
    - **d.** grandiose

11. planting a few red flowers here and there among the white flowers
    - **a.** subjugate
    - **b.** intersperse
    - **c.** extrapolate
    - **d.** transcend

12. predicting the hottest Christmas toy based on a phone survey
    - **a.** transgress
    - **b.** transcend
    - **c.** subjugate
    - **d.** extrapolate

13. devotion to religion
    - **a.** paucity
    - **b.** piety
    - **c.** levitation
    - **d.** proliferation

14. a magician's ability to make things appear to float
    - **a.** levitation
    - **b.** laceration
    - **c.** paucity
    - **d.** piety

15. a preference for one type of music over another
    - **a.** proliferation
    - **b.** viability
    - **c.** propensity
    - **d.** legibility

Vocabulary Power

Test: Unit 4

PART A

Circle the word that best completes each sentence.

1. From the positive reports of all ten exchange students in the program, we can _____ that future exchange students will also have a positive experience.

   a. subjugate   **b.** transcend   **c.** extrapolate   **d.** trangress

2. Letitia knew that in college _____ would be her worst enemy.

   a. piety   **b.** procrastination   **c.** levitation   **d.** enmity

3. The doctor reported that the _____ of white blood cells was a response to the medication.

   a. legibility   **b.** propensity   **c.** laceration   **d.** proliferation

4. After years of war, the people of the two nations felt only mistrust and _____ for each other.

   a. enmity   **b.** viability   **c.** propensity   **d.** obfuscation

5. When the judge learned that the man was suing his neighbor because leaves from the trees next door had blown onto his lawn, he tossed out the _____ lawsuit.

   a. ingenious   **b.** extravagant   **c.** frivolous   **d.** subservient

6. Several council members questioned the _____ of the proposal to build a bypass around the town because of strong public opinion against it.

   a. proliferation   **b.** piety   **c.** enmity   **d.** viability

7. The manufacturer makes an _____ claim for the product; the label says it will allow any bald man to grow back a full head of hair.

   a. opportune   **b.** extravagant   **c.** inept   **d.** ingenious

8. If you _____ the rule about staying out after 11:00 P.M., you will be grounded.

   a. intersperse   **b.** transgress   **c.** transcend   **d.** extrapolate

PART B

Circle the letter of the correct definition for each vocabulary word.

1. **obfuscation**

   a. elimination   **c.** delay

   b. confusion   **d.** obstruction

2. **inept**

   a. closed   **c.** pushy

   b. clumsy   **d.** narrow

3. **transcend**

   a. rise above

   b. break a rule

   c. conquer

   d. negotiate

4. **paucity**

   a. readability

   b. ability to live independently

   c. religious devotion

   d. few in number

5. **adroit**

   a. clumsy

   b. amoral

   c. clean

   d. skillful

6. **ingenious**

   a. grand

   b. clever

   c. timely

   d. strange

7. **superfluous**

   a. slavish

   b. flowing

   c. unnecessary

   d. extreme

8. **levitation**

   a. a rising into the air

   b. a minor wound

   c. humor

   d. careful thinking

9. **enmity**

   a. inequality

   b. hatred

   c. cheerfulness

   d. patience

10. **intermediary**

   a. satellite

   b. moderator

   c. assistant

   d. go-between

11. **opportune**

   a. timely

   b. silly

   c. conquering

   d. readable

12. **intersperse**

   a. travel

   b. delay

   c. bring to the front

   d. varying placement

Vocabulary Power

Lesson 17   Using Synonyms

Open any magazine or newspaper and you're likely to find an example of criticism or satire. People love to praise and point out flaws in human behavior. People react to the things they like and don't like, the things that shock, amuse, or anger them. The words in this list relate to criticism and satire.

Word List

conjecture	deference	insipid	sustenance
contention	derisive	laudable	
cursory	impartial	mirth	

EXERCISE A Synonyms

Each boldfaced vocabulary word is paired with a synonym whose meaning you probably know. Think of other words related to the synonym and write your ideas on the line provided. Then, look up the vocabulary word in a dictionary and write its definition.

1. **cursory** : hasty _____

   Dictionary definition _____

2. **deference** : submission _____

   Dictionary definition _____

3. **insipid** : flavorless _____

   Dictionary definition _____

4. **contention** : assertion _____

   Dictionary definition _____

5. **laudable** : praiseworthy _____

   Dictionary definition _____

6. **sustenance** : food _____

   Dictionary definition _____

7. **conjecture** : guess _____

   Dictionary definition _____

8. **impartial** : fair _____

   Dictionary definition _____

9. **derisive** : scornful _____

   Dictionary definition _____

10. **mirth** : laughter _____

    Dictionary definition _____

Vocabulary Power continued

EXERCISE B Clues Matching

Write the vocabulary word that best matches each clue.

1. describing a comedy routine built on stale jokes _____

2. describing the clean-up action in a neighborhood park _____

3. the belief that life exists outside Earth's galaxy _____

4. respect for the judgment of your boss _____

5. describing a remark made with a laugh and a sneer _____

6. requirement for physical survival _____

7. describing a quick glance at the headlines in the newspaper _____

8. claim made by nuclear agencies that their power plants are safe _____

9. reaction of young children to a clown's antics _____

10. describing the comparison of two brands of fruit drink by blindfolded tasters _____

EXERCISE C Antonyms

Write the vocabulary word that is most nearly *opposite* in meaning.

1. blameworthy _____

2. sparkling _____

3. prejudiced _____

4. thorough _____

5. sadness _____

6. respectful _____

7. poison _____

8. cooperation _____

9. condescension _____

10. known fact _____

Vocabulary Power

Lesson 18   The Word Roots *morph, flu/fluct/flux, tact/tang/tig, prehend/prehens*

The root is the basic part of a word that carries its main meaning. Many words in the English language, including those in the Word List, have Latin roots. Listed below are five useful Latin roots, with an example for each.

Root	Meaning	Example	Definition
flu, fluct, flux	flow	**influx**	a flowing in
morph	form, shape	**morphology**	study of form and structure of plants and animals
prehend, prehens	take, seize	**apprehend**	grasp, understand
tact, tang, tig	touch	**tactile**	referring to the sense of touch

Word List

amorphous	**fluctuate**	**reprehensible**	**tangential**
contiguous	**metamorphosis**	**tactful**	**tangible**
effluent	**prehensile**		

EXERCISE A   Roots and Meanings

Write the root contained in each boldfaced word. Then, look up the word in a dictionary and write its definition.

1. **effluent** _____

   Dictionary definition _____

2. **tangible** _____

   Dictionary definition _____

3. **tangential** _____

   Dictionary definition _____

4. **prehensile** _____

   Dictionary definition _____

5. **amorphous** _____

   Dictionary definition _____

6. **tactful** _____

   Dictionary definition _____

7. **fluctuate** _____

   Dictionary definition _____

Vocabulary Power continued

8. contiguous _____

   Dictionary definition _____

9. reprehensible _____

   Dictionary definition _____

10. metamorphosis _____

    Dictionary definition _____

EXERCISE B Sentence Completion

Write the vocabulary word that best completes each sentence.

1. Hawaii and Alaska are not part of the _____ United States.

2. The crowds at the summer concerts _____ depending on who is performing.

3. An opossum can hang from a tree branch by its _____ tail.

4. The blueberry stains on the culprit's fingers were the _____ evidence of his guilt.

5. Stuffing the ballot box on Election Day is an example of _____ conduct.

6. The _____ from the sewage treatment plant is harmful to fish in the river.

7. Christa's ability to be _____ made her an excellent diplomat.

8. The _____ of a caterpillar into a butterfly is one of the wonders of nature.

9. Marta had only a(n) _____ involvement with the club; she attended meetings twice a year.

10. In the potter's hands, the _____ lump of clay became a finely shaped bowl.

EXERCISE C Word Web

On a separate sheet of paper, create a word web for one of the roots used in this lesson. With a partner, brainstorm or use a dictionary to come up with words for your word web. In the dictionary entry for the word, check the origin to make sure the word contains the correct root.

Vocabulary Power

Lesson 19   The Prefixes *im-*, *in-*, and *un-*

A prefix is a word part attached at the beginning of a word or root. The prefixes *im-*, *in-*, and *un-* all mean "not." Adding a prefix to a word modifies its meaning. For example, the word *illiterate (il + literate)* means "not able to read or write."

Word List

immaculate	implausible	infallible	unprecedented
imperturbable	incongruous	unobtrusive	unpretentious
impervious	indiscriminate		

EXERCISE A Definitions

Each boldfaced vocabulary word is followed by a brief definition that emphasizes the meaning of the prefix and the root or base word. Look up the word in a dictionary and write its definition.

1. **imperturbable** : not disturbable

   Dictionary definition _____

2. **unpretentious** : not showy

   Dictionary definition _____

3. **infallible** : not erring

   Dictionary definition _____

4. **immaculate** : not blemished

   Dictionary definition _____

5. **unobtrusive** : not standing out

   Dictionary definition _____

6. **indiscriminate** : not making distinctions

   Dictionary definition _____

7. **impervious** : not open to passage

   Dictionary definition _____

8. **incongruous** : not in harmony

   Dictionary definition _____

9. **unprecedented** : not done before

   Dictionary definition _____

10. **implausible** : not believable

    Dictionary definition _____

Vocabulary Power *continued*

EXERCISE B Antonyms

Write the vocabulary word that is an antonym for each of the following words.

1. _____ harmonious

2. error-prone
   noticeable _____

3. _____ careful

4. expected
   believable _____

5. excitable _____

_____ 6. filthy

_____ 7.

_____ 8. open

_____ 9.

_____ 10. showy

EXERCISE C Usage

If the boldfaced word is used correctly in the sentence, write *correct* above it. If not, draw a line through it and write the correct vocabulary word above it.

1. The tractor, covered with a plastic sheet that was **infallible** to rain and snow, remained dry and rust-free.

2. I'm not **immaculate**; like everyone else, I make mistakes.

3. The cloning experiment that created Dolly the sheep was **unpretentious**; never before had an adult mammal given birth to a genetic copy of itself.

4. The huge wolfhound looked **incongruous** lined up with the eight miniature poodles.

5. While the squealing children ran around the room, the **imperturbable** baby-sitter calmly worked on her algebra assignment.

6. The **unobtrusive** observer sat in the last row of the classroom and spoke to no one.

7. Although he is a millionaire, he lives in an **indiscriminate** three-room apartment and has a modest lifestyle.

8. Her prediction that some day all cars would run on corn fuel seemed **implausible** to me.

9. She made sure her clothes were pressed and **infallible** for the debutant ball.

10. Her lifelong habit of **indiscriminate** sunbathing had done terrible damage to her skin.

Vocabulary Power

Lesson 20   Using Reference Skills
Using a Dictionary: Multiple-Meaning Words

In using a dictionary, you've noticed that many words have more than one meaning. These different meanings are numbered with the most common meaning being given first. Use the dictionary entry for the word *index* to answer the questions below.

> **index** (in′ deks) *n.* **1.** Something that serves to guide or point out, especially: **a.** An alphabetized list of names, places, and subjects treated in a printed work, giving the page(s) on which each item is mentioned **b.** A thumb index **c.** A table, file, or catalog **2.** Something that reveals or indicates; a sign **3.** An indicator or pointer, as on a scientific instrument **4.** *Mathematics.* **a.** A number or symbol, often written as a subscript or superscript to a mathematical expression, that indicates an operation to be performed **b.** A number derived from a formula, used to characterize a set of data

EXERCISE

Read each sentence. Then, from the entry above, write the meaning of *index* that fits the sentence.

1. The consumer price **index**, known as the CPI, measures the average change in the prices of goods and services purchased for day-to-day living.

   Meaning of *index* _____

2. Her facial expression was an **index** of her mood.

   Meaning of *index* _____

3. When I looked up "Charlemagne" in the **index** of my history textbook, I was referred to page 472 for a description of his reign.

   Meaning of *index* _____

4. The librarian directed me to this Web site for an **index** to publications of the U.S. Government.

   Meaning of *index* _____

5. The **index** on the sundial cast a sharp shadow; from it, I estimated that the time was three o'clock in the afternoon.

   Meaning of *index* _____

6. In the mathematical expression x^{10}, the **index** 10 indicates that you should multiply *x* by itself 10 times.

   Meaning of *index* _____

Vocabulary Power

Review: Unit 5

EXERCISE

Circle the word in parentheses that best completes each sentence.

1. All members of the jury must be fair and (impervious, impartial, implausible).

2. His performance was (implausible, laudable, insipid) even though he did not win the race.

3. In the debate, his main (contention, deference, conjecture) was that immigrants are an asset to the nation.

4. Keeshia was (immaculate, indiscriminate, incongruous) in choosing her daily wardrobe; she grabbed the first outfit she saw.

5. In (sustenance, deference, conjecture) to her grandmother's wishes, Mia always closed the door to her room before practicing her clarinet.

6. I know Pete finds Saturday morning cartoons (impartial, infallible, insipid) because he said, "There's nothing original or exciting about them."

7. Monkeys have (reprehensible, prehensile, cursory) hands and feet that allow them to grasp and swing from branches.

8. The sign is (unpretentious, unobtrusive, unprecedented) because it is small and painted to blend in with the surroundings.

9. Kevin's car is always in (impartial, imperturbable, immaculate) condition; he washes and waxes it every Saturday.

10. Alaska is not part of the (contiguous, amorphous, effluent) United States.

11. The results of the fundraiser for new computers were (unprecedented, impervious, tangential) in the history of our school.

12. To be a successful manager, you must be (amorphous, incongruous, tactful) and succint.

13. My favorite science fiction movie has a(n) (indiscriminate, insipid, amorphous) character with shape-changing abilities.

14. The halls echoed with students' (sustenance, mirth, contentions) as they prepared for summer vacation.

15. We purchased the house by a beautiful, (cursory, infallible, effluent) stream.

Vocabulary Power

Test: Unit 5

PART A

Circle the letter of the correct definition for each vocabulary word.

1. fluctuate
   - **a.** rise and fall, as in waves
   - **b.** travel back and forth
   - **c.** flow out of
   - **d.** clarify

2. sustenance
   - **a.** greed
   - **b.** flexibility
   - **c.** laughter
   - **d.** food

3. cursory
   - **a.** admirable
   - **b.** cruel
   - **c.** roundabout
   - **d.** hasty

4. contention
   - **a.** guess
   - **b.** fenced area
   - **c.** defense
   - **d.** assertion

5. reprehensible
   - **a.** blameworthy
   - **b.** grasping
   - **c.** erroneous
   - **d.** irrational

6. metamorphosis
   - **a.** thoughtfulness
   - **b.** delay
   - **c.** transformation
   - **d.** shape

7. immaculate
   - **a.** very late
   - **b.** pure
   - **c.** irregular
   - **d.** unbelievable

8. indiscriminate
   - **a.** prejudiced
   - **b.** careless
   - **c.** intolerable
   - **d.** boring

9. imperturbable
   - **a.** irritable
   - **b.** calm
   - **c.** disappointed
   - **d.** concrete

10. laudable
   - **a.** silly
   - **b.** worthy of praise
   - **c.** able to be heard
   - **d.** heavy

PART B

Circle the letter of the word that best completes each sentence.

1. The article's claim that milk is harmful to people's health seems _____ to Martin.
   - **a.** impartial
   - **b.** cursory
   - **c.** implausible
   - **d.** amorphous

2. During our discussion of the chemistry experiment, Fred made many _____ remarks about last night's football game.
   - **a.** contiguous
   - **b.** incongruous
   - **c.** reprehensible
   - **d.** tangible

Vocabulary Power *continued*

3. Medieval footsoldiers carried shields that were _____ to arrows.
   a. impervious   **b.** infallible   **c.** imperturbable   **d.** unobtrusive

4. My plans for the summer are still somewhat _____; I have no definite plans yet.
   a. insipid   **b.** laudable   **c.** effluent   **d.** amorphous

5. Angry members of the crowd interrupted the speaker with _____ remarks.
   a. derisive   **b.** impartial   **c.** tangible   **d.** tactful

6. There was a(n) _____ lack of respect for the speaker evident as the murmur grew louder as he spoke.
   a. contiguous   **b.** tangible   **c.** impartial   **d.** unpretentious

7. Out of _____ to his parents, Peter made curfew.
   a. sustenance   **b.** mirth   **c.** contention   **d.** deference

8. His _____ whining made everyone walk away when he tried to talk to them.
   a. laudable   **b.** immaculate   **c.** insipid   **d.** infallible

9. Nancy's _____ that the car repair had been completed haphazardly proved correct when the bumper fell off.
   a. conjecture   **b.** mirth   **c.** sustenance   **d.** metamorphosis

10. The case brought against the taxi driver was _____ in our little town of Bufort, Illinois.
    a. immaculate   **b.** prehensile   **c.** infallible   **d.** unprecedented

11. His lecture on alligators in algebra class was very _____.
    a. tangential   **b.** laudable   **c.** imperturbable   **d.** unobtrusive

12. Jane decided to just make a(n) _____ examination of her essay test before handing it in.
    a. effluent   **b.** unobtrusive   **c.** cursory   **d.** tactful

13. We will not accept such _____ behavior in our school!
    a. impartial   **b.** reprehensible   **c.** unpretentious   **d.** immaculate

14. This new system for detecting fires is _____; it has never failed in laboratory tests.
    a. laudable   **b.** reprehensible   **c.** contiguous   **d.** infallible

15. I don't enjoy the way temperatures _____ a lot in the spring and fall.
    a. sustain   **b.** defer   **c.** contend   **d.** fluctuate

Vocabulary Power

Lesson 21   Using Synonyms

"It was the best of times, it was the worst of times. . . ." In this famous first line from *A Tale of Two Cities,* Charles Dickens sums up the era of the French Revolution in France and England. Could these words describe a time in American history too? Could they describe the present rather than the past? The words in this list can help you write and talk about the best and worst times of your life.

> **Word List**
>
> | | | | |
> |---|---|---|---|
> | coerce | epiphany | feign | predilection |
> | disconcerting | exacerbate | precept | temper |
> | droll | exhort | | |

EXERCISE A   Synonyms

Each boldfaced vocabulary word is paired with a synonym whose meaning you probably know. Think of other related words and write your ideas on the line. Then, look up the vocabulary word in a dictionary and write its meaning.

1. **feign:** pretend _____

   Dictionary definition _____

2. **disconcerting:** disturbing _____

   Dictionary definition _____

3. **epiphany:** insight _____

   Dictionary definition _____

4. **predilection:** preference _____

   Dictionary definition _____

5. **coerce:** force _____

   Dictionary definition _____

6. **exhort:** advise _____

   Dictionary definition _____

7. **exacerbate:** worsen _____

   Dictionary definition _____

8. **temper:** moderate _____

   Dictionary definition _____

9. **precept:** rule _____

   Dictionary definition _____

10. **droll:** amusing _____

    Dictionary definition _____

Vocabulary Power continued

EXERCISE B Usage

Answer each question with an explanation. Use your understanding of the boldfaced word in your answer.

1. Would a **droll** person be fun to spend time with?

   _____

2. Could someone **coerce** you to go to a movie?

   _____

3. What could **exacerbate** being stranded on the ocean in a rowboat?

   _____

4. What does it mean to **temper** justice with mercy?

   _____

5. Could discovering that your shirt is on inside out be **disconcerting?**

   _____

EXERCISE C Clues Matching

Write the vocabulary word that fits each clue.

1. make a show of not caring about something when you really do _____

2. advise a young chess player to practice at least one hour a day _____

3. a liking for jazz more than other kinds of music _____

4. always treat others as you wish to be treated _____

5. the sudden understanding of a difficult concept _____

6. compel a friend to do something he really does not want to do _____

7. moderate a volatile situation _____

8. having a conversation with Sally then realizing it's her twin Sue _____

9. calling in sick for work, being seen at the mall, and lying about it _____

10. an entertaining sketch by a comic _____

Vocabulary Power

Lesson 22 Suffixes That Form Adjectives

A suffix is a word ending that can be added to a word or root. The suffix often indicates the word's part of speech. Listed below are some adjectival suffixes. Knowing their meaning can help you understand unfamiliar words. The Word List supplies sample words.

Suffix	Meaning	Example	Definition
-able	able, capable of	admissible	able to be admitted
-al	of or relating to	dental	relating to the teeth
-ent	promoting or causing an action	absorbent	promoting absorption
-ic	of or relating to	organic	relating to the organs of the body
-ious	full of, marked by	delicious	marked by delight; very pleasant

Word List

affable	detrimental	laconic	propitious
caustic	evanescent	ostentatious	unfathomable
convivial	expedient		

EXERCISE A Suffixes

Underline the suffix in each word. Then, look up the word in a dictionary and write its definition.

1. expedient _____

2. unfathomable _____

3. detrimental _____

4. convivial _____

5. affable _____

6. ostentatious _____

7. laconic _____

8. evanescent _____

9. caustic _____

10. propitious _____

Vocabulary Power continued

EXERCISE B Usage

Answer each question using your understanding of the boldfaced word.

1. What might an **ostentatious** house look like on the inside? _____

_____

2. How long might an **evanescent** rainbow last? _____

_____

3. How might an **affable** person greet you? _____

_____

4. What habit is considered **detrimental** to your health? _____

_____

5. What might a **caustic** chemical do to your skin? _____

_____

6. What would be a **propitious** time for an outdoor picnic? _____

_____

7. If a party was **convivial,** what would it be like? _____

_____

8. If you acted in an **expedient** manner, would others respect you? _____

_____

9. If a person's answer was **unfathomable,** what could you learn from it? _____

_____

10. If you tried to converse with a **laconic** person, how might the person respond? _____

_____

Vocabulary Power

Lesson 23   The Word Roots *cred, ten*

The root is the basic part of a word that carries its main meaning. Many words in the English language have Latin roots. Two common Latin roots are listed in the chart, with a word example for each. The Word List supplies other examples.

Root	Meaning	Example	Definition
cred	believe	credible	believable
ten	stretch, hold, thin	tension	force that tends to stretch something; mental strain

Word List

credibility	discredit	ostensible	tenuous
creditable	extenuating	tenet	tenure
credo	incredulous		

EXERCISE A   Roots

Underline the root contained in each word. Then, look up the word and write its definition.

1. credo _____

2. tenuous _____

3. credibility _____

4. extenuating _____

5. discredit _____

6. tenure _____

7. creditable _____

8. ostensible _____

9. incredulous _____

10. tenet _____

EXERCISE B   Usage

If the boldfaced word is used correctly in the sentence, write *correct* above it. If not, draw a line through it and write the correct vocabulary word above it.

1. The **ostensible** purpose of the trip was to attend a meeting, but he had other reasons for going to Hawaii.

2. "Do no harm" is a **tenure** of the medical profession.

3. Because of the **extenuating** circumstance of getting a flat tire, we can't blame Hank for being late.

Vocabulary Power continued

4. During his **tenet** as president of the club, he accomplished a great deal.

5. When we told Maria that a truck had just delivered an elephant to her house, she was **incredulous**.

6. Her **tenure** as a journalist has been helped by her honest, hard-hitting reporting style.

7. The company's hold on its employees was **tenuous** because of the low pay.

8. One of the club's **credibilities** is a belief in being kind to strangers.

9. His attempt to **discredit** the politician was completely successful.

10. Sally was pleasantly surprised by how **creditable** the video made her look.

EXERCISE C Multiple-Meaning Words

Some words have several related definitions listed within a single dictionary entry. Each meaning, however, is based on the meaning of the word root. The word *creditable,* for example, is from the Latin root *credere,* meaning "to believe." A dictionary entry for *creditable* lists four different meanings, but all of them are related to the root meaning "to believe." Use a dictionary to help you write the precise definition of *creditable* as it is used in each sentence below.

1. Her 1987 car was not accepted as **creditable** collateral for the loan.

   Definition _____

2. The *Times* reporter did a **creditable** job of exposing graft in city hall.

   Definition _____

3. Dean Jackson did not approve the five-page paper as a **creditable** class requirement.

   Definition _____

4. The mayor proposed a **creditable** argument for building the bridge.

   Definition _____

Vocabulary Power

Lesson 24   Using Reading Skills
Learning from Context: Comparison and Contrast

When you encounter an unfamiliar word in your reading, you can often deduce its meaning from the context. Two useful context clues are *comparison* and *contrast*. A comparison is often signaled by words such as *like, same,* and *too.* A contrast may be signaled by words such as *but, however,* and *not.* Study the two examples below.

> Comparison: You look *hale*, and your sister looks healthy too.
> Analysis: Because of the comparison clue *too* and the word *healthy*, you can deduce that *hale* means "healthy."
>
> Contrast: The original manuscript of the author's best-known novel is *extant*, but all of her other manuscripts have been lost or destroyed.
> Analysis: Because of the contrast clue *but* and the words *lost or destroyed,* you can deduce that *extant* means "not lost or destroyed" or "still in existence."

EXERCISE A

In each sentence, circle the word or words that signal a comparison or contrast. Then, on the basis of the context clues, write the likely meaning of the boldfaced word.

1. Like the poetry of Edgar Allan Poe, which often dwells on death, Stephen King's novels tend to be **macabre.**

   _____

2. Product Y claims to be a **panacea,** and product X is likewise advertised as a cure-all.

   _____

3. Unlike my **querulous** neighbor upstairs, my downstairs neighbor never complains when I practice piano.

   _____

4. The **genre** of literature known as science fiction is similar to the literary category of fantasy.

   _____

5. Like an orange, the **kumquat** has a thick rind, but, unlike an orange, it is small and oval.

   _____

6. I'm nothing like my **bumptious** cousin; whether with friends or strangers, I'm never pushy.

   _____

EXERCISE B

Look up the boldfaced words in Exercise A in a dictionary and write their definitions on a separate sheet of paper. Then, select three of the words and write a sentence using each.

Vocabulary Power

Review: Unit 6

EXERCISE A

Circle the word that best completes each sentence.

1. It's difficult to (feign, exhort, temper) enthusiasm if you are not really excited.

2. Ursula really dislikes opera, so I won't (coerce, exacerbate, temper) her to attend *Rigoletto* with me.

3. Using made-up quotations in an article will (exhort, discredit, feign) any journalist.

4. Jack found the sudden interruption of his speech very (disconcerting, ostensible, incredulous).

5. James enjoys tacos and enchiladas, but Miriam has a (predilection, credo, tenure) for stir-fried food.

6. Not getting enough sleep is (disconcerting, affable, detrimental) to a person's performance at school and at work.

7. The reasons you have for leaving are (droll, unfathomable, affable) to me, they don't make sense.

8. Her hold on the cliff face is (tenuous, laconic, disconcerting) at best—we must rescue her now!

9. The police believe that there are (propitious, extenuating, disconcerting) circumstances in this kidnapping case.

10. Using e-mail is often the most (evanescent, incredulous, expedient) way to communicate.

EXERCISE B

Cross out the word that does not belong in each word group.

1. droll, affable, ostensible, convivial

2. precept, temper, tenet, credo

3. detrimental, caustic, disconcerting, convivial

4. unfathomable, affable, incredulous, disconcerting

5. epiphany, discredit, exhort, coerce

Vocabulary Power

Test: Unit 6

PART A

Circle the letter of the synonym for each boldfaced word.

1. **predilection**
   a. prediction b. preference c. preview d. premonition

2. **coerce**
   a. trace b. create c. force d. lead

3. **incredulous**
   a. believable b. unbelievable c. sad d. angry

4. **tenuous**
   a. tense b. flimsy c. amusing d. stressful

5. **feign**
   a. pretend b. fall c. rule d. speak

6. **disconcerting**
   a. damaging b. unmusical c. confusing d. calming

7. **droll**
   a. burning b. moderate c. amusing d. stale

8. **precept**
   a. predilection b. square c. tenet d. tenure

PART B

Circle the letter of the word that fits each example.

1. belief that all people are created equal
   a. tenet b. tenure c. credibility d. precept

2. describing a person of few words
   a. laconic b. affable c. droll d. expedient

3. describing action taken to get the job done
   a. expedient b. extenuating c. convivial d. evanescent

4. period during which a person was president of a university
   a. tenet b. tenure c. credo d. precept

5. circumstances that would cause a jury to give less than the maximum sentence to a convicted criminal
   a. expedient b. extenuating c. convivial d. evanescent

Vocabulary Power *continued*

6. the effect of drinking alcohol on a person's ability to drive safely
   a. evanescent   **b.** laconic   **c.** detrimental   **d.** creditable

7. describing a surprise birthday party at which everyone had a good time
   a. ostentatious   **b.** caustic   **c.** convivial   **d.** droll

PART C

Circle the letter of the correct definition of each vocabulary word.

1. **discredit**
   a. disguise the appearance of   **c.** charge too much for a purchase
   b. damage the reputation of   **d.** receive a refund

2. **temper**
   a. become irritable   **c.** pretend
   b. make milder   **d.** cause a delay

3. **exhort**
   a. skip out   **c.** speak loudly
   b. dig out   **d.** urge strongly

4. **ostensible**
   a. open to view   **c.** excusable
   b. boastfully showy   **d.** using few words

5. **caustic**
   a. harmful to one's health   **c.** capable of burning by chemical action
   b. serving as the reason for something   **d.** helpful to the community

Vocabulary Power

Lesson 25   Word Usage

When you choose a movie or book, do you prefer stories about everyday life or about fantastic places and events? Both kinds of stories can stir our emotions, from anger and fear to love and courage. Other forms of human expression, including music, art, and dance, also move us emotionally. To which of these forms do you respond most deeply? The words in this list relate to the expression of feelings.

Word List

abyss	deluge	piquant	plaintive
acute	faculty	placid	reverie
aesthetic	illustrious		

EXERCISE A **Synonyms**

Each boldfaced word is paired with a synonym whose meaning you probably know. Think of other words related to the synonym and write them on the line provided. Then, look up each vocabulary word in a dictionary and write its meaning.

1. **placid** : calm _____

   Dictionary definition _____

2. **illustrious** : outstanding _____

   Dictionary definition _____

3. **abyss** : pit _____

   Dictionary definition _____

4. **reverie** : daydream _____

   Dictionary definition _____

5. **faculty** : ability _____

   Dictionary definition _____

6. **aesthetic** : artistic _____

   Dictionary definition _____

7. **deluge** : flood _____

   Dictionary definition _____

8. **piquant** : spicy _____

   Dictionary definition _____

9. **acute** : sharp _____

   Dictionary definition _____

10. **plaintive** : sorrowful _____

    Dictionary definition _____

Vocabulary Power *continued*

EXERCISE B Usage

Draw a line through the italicized phrase and, above it, write the vocabulary word that is appropriate.

1. The roast turkey was served with a(n) *pleasantly spicy* sauce made of cranberries and onions.

2. The slamming of the back door jolted her out of her *daydream.*

3. After suffering a stroke, Mr. Johnson had an impaired *power* of speech.

4. Winifred gasped as the keys to the car fell into the bottomless *gulf.*

5. A(n) *overwhelming flood* of letters poured into the senator's office after he voted against the health-care bill.

EXERCISE C Multiple-Meaning Words

Many words in English have more than one meaning. Each meaning, however, is based on the meaning of the word root. The word *faculty*, for example, is from the Latin root *facilis*, meaning "easy." A dictionary entry for *faculty* lists many different meanings, but all of them are related to the root meaning "easy." Use a dictionary to help you write the precise definition of *faculty* as it is used in each sentence below.

1. In the pitch dark, he counted on his **faculty** of hearing to guide him to the intruder.

   Definition _____

2. That comedian has the **faculty** of delivering perfectly timed punch lines.

   Definition _____

3. After a period of training, the clergy member received **faculties** for administering the last rites.

   Definition _____

4. Our high-school **faculty** numbers eight women and six men.

   Definition _____

EXERCISE D Derivations

Use a dictionary to find out which two vocabulary words in the list are derived from the French language. Write the words on the line.

_____

Vocabulary Power

Lesson 26   Word Root *gen*

The root is the basic part of a word that carries its main meaning. Many words in the English language have Latin roots. All of the words in the list below contain the root *gen,* meaning "give birth." You probably already know a number of words that contain this root, such as *general, gentle, gender,* and *genuine.* Words made from the *gen* root come from a large family of words that is derived from several related roots that refer to pro-creation or to family and tribal groups.

Word List

congenial	genocide	heterogeneous	indigenous
generic	genre	homogeneous	ingenuous
genesis	genteel		

EXERCISE A   Roots and Meanings

Each boldfaced word is followed by a definition that emphasizes the meaning of the root. Look up the word in a dictionary and write the more exact meaning. Include a synonym if one is given.

1. **generic:** describing an entire group

   Dictionary definition _____

2. **indigenous:** connected to a specific place by birth

   Dictionary definition _____

3. **genesis:** the coming into being of something

   Dictionary definition _____

4. **homogeneous:** of the same kind

   Dictionary definition _____

5. **heterogeneous:** of different kinds

   Dictionary definition _____

6. **congenial:** having the same tastes or habits

   Dictionary definition _____

7. **ingenuous:** showing childlike simplicity and frankness

   Dictionary definition _____

8. **genocide:** killing off of an entire nation or ethnic group

   Dictionary definition _____

9. **genre:** kind or sort

   Dictionary definition _____

10. **genteel:** having a polite or an aristocratic manner

    Dictionary definition _____

Vocabulary Power continued

EXERCISE B · Word Association

Write the vocabulary word that belongs in each group of words.

1. refined, elegant, polite   _____

2. kind, type, category   _____

3. diverse, dissimilar, varied   _____

4. frank, open, childlike   _____

5. agreeable, friendly, sociable   _____

6. same, similar, uniform   _____

EXERCISE C · Usage

If the boldfaced word is used correctly in the sentence, write *correct* above it. If not, draw a line through it and write the correct vocabulary word above it.

1. The German Nazi government's attempt to exterminate the Jews during World War II is one of the most infamous examples of **genocide.**

2. The ladybugs that are so numerous this spring are not **ingenuous;** they were brought into the United States from Germany.

3. When asked about the **genesis** of the Special Olympics, Dan explained how the athletic competition for mentally and physically disabled persons came into being.

4. The formula for a **genteel** prescription drug is the same as for a specific brand, but the drug costs less.

5. That band sure looks **heterogeneous,** with everyone wearing red wigs and yellow uniforms.

6. *Tom Sawyer* is classified in the **genre** of adventure stories.

7. Lauren's **genteel** grandmother graciously welcomed us for the weekend.

8. The crowd that gathered for the new mall's opening was definitely **homogeneous.**

9. His fumbling attempts to ask me on a date were endearing and **indigenous.**

10. Susan was voted most **congenial** in her class.

Vocabulary Power

Lesson 27   The Prefix *trans-*

A prefix is a word part attached at the beginning of a word or root. The prefix *trans-* means "across" or "beyond." Adding a prefix to a base word or root modifies its meaning. For example, the word *transmit* means "send across." The ten words in the list below all contain the prefix *trans-*.

Word List

transfigure	transient	transmute	transpose
transfix	transition	transpire	transverse
transfusion	transmogrify		

EXERCISE A   Word Clues

Each phrase contains a clue about the meaning of the word. Make a guess about the meaning of the boldfaced word within its context. Then, look up the word in a dictionary and write its definition.

1. **transverse** beam in a ceiling _____

   Dictionary definition _____

2. **transition** from fall to winter _____

   Dictionary definition _____

3. **transfix** someone with a stare _____

   Dictionary definition _____

4. a **transient** crush on someone _____

   Dictionary definition _____

5. plants which **transpire** water vapor _____

   Dictionary definition _____

6. **transpose** two letters in a misspelled word _____

   Dictionary definition _____

7. **transfigure** a legendary hero _____

   Dictionary definition _____

8. a blood **transfusion** in a hospital _____

   Dictionary definition _____

9. **transmute** water into vapor _____

   Dictionary definition _____

Vocabulary Power *continued*

10. **transmogrify** from a mouse into a monster _____

   Dictionary definition _____

EXERCISE B   Sentence Completion
Complete the sentence using the most appropriate vocabulary word.

1. The apples in these orchards are picked by _____ workers, who are here for only about two weeks and then move on.

2. Medieval alchemists believed that it was possible to _____ lead into gold.

3. According to some, commercial development will _____ the pleasant avenue into an ugly shopping strip.

4. The arrival of the McCanns brought a _____ of merriment to the dull party.

5. _____ canyons occur when rivers cut across existing gorges.

6. Good deeds seemed to _____ the young man into a wise statesman.

7. After reviewing a list of her goals, Evelyn decided to _____ the third and fourth goals.

8. The magician was always able to _____ the crowd with his amazing final trick.

9. Not knowing what might _____, the musician paced outside the recording studio.

10. In the musical, a brief flute solo provides a _____ from the spirited chorus to the moving duet between the two lovers.

Vocabulary Power

Vocabulary Power

Lesson 28   Using Reading Skills
Learning from Context

When you are reading and come across an unfamiliar word, you can often use the surrounding words, or context, to figure out the meaning. Sometimes you may find a cause-and-effect clue in the context. A statement of cause and effect is often signaled by clue words such as *because, therefore, since, so, consequently,* and *as a result of.*

Cause and Effect
Because of the opaque window shades, almost no daylight entered the room.
<u>Analysis</u>: Using the clue word *because*, you could figure out that the opaque shades caused the darkness in the room. Thus, *opaque* could mean "able to block light."

EXERCISE

In each sentence, underline the word or words that signal cause or effect. Then, on the basis of the context clue, circle the likely meaning of the boldfaced word.

1. The new invention was a **debacle,** so the inventor had to try a totally new approach to solving the problem. (great success, complete failure, partial success)

2. Jerome woke up in a **churlish** mood; consequently, he was rude to everyone. (irritable, humorous, selfish)

3. Because Nell is so **loquacious,** my ear throbbed after I got off the telephone with her. (friendly, talkative, grateful)

4. Since the aim of this organization is to **ameliorate** the living conditions of the poor, it offers free clothing and adult tutoring in English. (eliminate, improve, stretch out)

5. I arrived at the party an hour late; as a result, my hostess gave me a **disparaging** look. (disapproving, welcoming, suspicious)

6. The program gives people a feeling of **efficacy** because they help to build their own homes. (tardiness, capability, paralysis)

7. Our father is a **paragon** of virtue, so we always seek his opinion about moral choices. (model, contradiction, coach)

8. Because Anna continually **chides** her about her choice of friends, Jessica rarely invites her to gatherings. (praises, teases, scolds)

Vocabulary Power

Review: Unit 7

EXERCISE

Circle the word that best completes each sentence.

1. For cooling, the human body needs to (transpose, transpire, transmute) liquid through the skin.

2. The books in this bookstore are organized by (genesis, reverie, genre).

3. We could hear the (piquant, plaintive, placid) cry of the lost puppy at the back door.

4. The main character in the novel sinks into a(n) (deluge, abyss, faculty) of crime and deception.

5. Purple loosestrife, not a(n) (indigenous, illustrious, homogeneous) plant in this area, tends to displace many native plants.

6. As a journalist, Benny is a(n) (acute, aesthetic, piquant) observer of life in this town.

7. The (genteel, placid, illustrious) mountain retreat was a wonderful place to escape the stresses of the city.

8. Because she has a tendency to (transmute, transfix, transpose) numbers, Dana would not be a good accountant.

9. A great (deluge, abyss, genre) poured into the streets after the dam broke.

10. Dylan has the (generic, genteel, acute) manners of a medieval knight.

11. The (genteel, acute, generic) brand of shampoo is just as good as the more expensive types.

12. The chicken breast is smothered in a(n) (piquant, placed, illustrious) sauce and served with steamed vegetables.

13. Bryan snapped out of his (deluge, reverie, faculty) about buying a motorcycle just as the light changed to green.

14. "The only thing that will save him now is a (transition, transfusion, deluge)," stated the doctor.

15. Robin grew tired of the (transient, acute, piquant) nature of her consulting job and looked for something permanent.

Vocabulary Power

Test: Unit 7

PART A
Circle the letter of the correct definition of each vocabulary word.

1. transpose
  a. reverse
  b. glorify
  c. guess
  d. change

2. deluge
  a. defeat
  b. flood
  c. sport
  d. delay

3. genocide
  a. killing of all plants
  b. killing of an entire family
  c. killing of injured livestock
  d. killing of an entire ethnic group

4. transfigure
  a. change the flow of
  b. change the state of
  c. change the calculation of
  d. change the feelings of

5. homogeneous
  a. dissimilar
  b. male
  c. uniform
  d. healthy

6. genesis
  a. religious feeling
  b. beginning
  c. membership in a group
  d. polite manner

7. transfix
  a. hold motionless in terror or wonder
  b. glue one thing to another
  c. change the order of
  d. correct an error

8. genteel
  a. very kind to animals
  b. extremely polite in manner
  c. very tender
  d. very aggressive

9. transmute
  a. change from one form into another
  b. become silent
  c. cross into another country
  d. damage or destroy

10. transpire
  a. die
  b. carry
  c. deceive
  d. give off vapor

Vocabulary Power *continued*

PART B

Circle the letter of the synonym for each word.

1. genre
   - **a.** topic
   - **b.** class
   - **c.** item
   - **d.** subject

2. ingenuous
   - **a.** insincere
   - **b.** fake
   - **c.** frank
   - **d.** mature

3. transient
   - **a.** native
   - **b.** passing
   - **c.** transparent
   - **d.** versatile

4. plaintive
   - **a.** narrow
   - **b.** melancholy
   - **c.** unadorned
   - **d.** contented

5. transpire
   - **a.** inhale
   - **b.** happen
   - **c.** reach
   - **d.** conclude

6. placid
   - **a.** calm
   - **b.** plain
   - **c.** icy
   - **d.** warm

7. abyss
   - **a.** peninsula
   - **b.** pit
   - **c.** tower
   - **d.** ocean

8. congenial
   - **a.** agreeable
   - **b.** cozy
   - **c.** inherited
   - **d.** unpleasant

9. reverie
   - **a.** inattention
   - **b.** alarm
   - **c.** swim
   - **d.** daydream

10. piquant
    - **a.** tasteless
    - **b.** moderate
    - **c.** temperate
    - **d.** pungent

11. transition
    - **a.** change
    - **b.** ageless
    - **c.** flexible
    - **d.** keep

12. generic
    - **a.** unique
    - **b.** controlled
    - **c.** common
    - **d.** grown

13. acute
    - **a.** polite
    - **b.** monetary
    - **c.** crucial
    - **d.** decent

14. illustrious
    - **a.** uncertain
    - **b.** renowned
    - **c.** absent
    - **d.** universal

15. indigenous
    - **a.** structure
    - **b.** repulsive
    - **c.** humble
    - **d.** innate

Vocabulary Power

Vocabulary Power

Lesson 29   Using Context Clues

Many writers have described the everlasting nature of truth and beauty. For example, William Shakespeare wrote, "Truth is truth / To the end of reckoning" (*Measure for Measure*), and John Keats wrote, "A thing of beauty is a joy forever" (*Endymion*). How would you describe truth and beauty? The words in this list could help you express your ideas.

Word List

connoisseur	enigma	inscrutable	refulgent
criterion	erudite	intangible	resplendent
edification	ineffable		

EXERCISE A   Context Clues

Read each sentence below and use context clues to guess the meaning of the boldfaced word. Write your definition; then, write the dictionary definition. If the dictionary lists more than one definition, choose the one that best fits the sentence.

1. Her face was **refulgent** with joy as the nurse placed her newborn in her arms.

   My definition _____

   Dictionary definition _____

2. The new car I saw at the dealership is **resplendent** with its glossy paint and polished bumpers.

   My definition _____

   Dictionary definition _____

3. This symphony, wonderful to hear, also has **intangible** qualities that appeal to the soul.

   My definition _____

   Dictionary definition _____

4. Rolf's parents sent him to Bible camp for religious **edification**; instead, he became an expert at trading baseball cards.

   My definition _____

   Dictionary definition _____

5. Cindy is a **connoisseur** of Japanese food and will eat only at restaurants with the best chefs.

   My definition _____

   Dictionary definition _____

6. We know that Stonehenge is an orderly grouping of enormous stone slabs in England, but exactly how and why prehistoric people constructed the monument remains an **enigma**.

   My definition _____

   Dictionary definition _____

Vocabulary Power *continued*

7. The artist's skillful use of paint strokes is one **criterion** an art critic uses to judge a painting.

   My definition _____

   Dictionary definition _____

8. Gary tried to write a sonnet about his girlfriend; but, when he couldn't think of any suitable words to describe how lovely she was, he decided that her beauty was **ineffable**.

   My definition _____

   Dictionary definition _____

9. Although the ancient language of the scroll was recognizable, the overall meaning was **inscrutable**.

   My definition _____

   Dictionary definition _____

10. Our English teacher is so **erudite** that he can teach any interdisciplinary course.

   My definition _____

   Dictionary definition _____

EXERCISE B   True or False

Read each sentence and decide whether it is true or false on the basis of the meaning of the boldfaced word. Write *true* or *false* and briefly explain your answer.

1. A **connoisseur** of sculpture would be most interested in the work of beginning art students.

   _____

2. Reading books, attending lectures, and making trips to museums can contribute to a person's **edification**.

   _____

3. The flavors, textures, and aromas of a well-prepared meal are **intangible** qualities.

   _____

4. An **erudite** person might know a lot about Chinese art but not about other topics.

   _____

5. Something described as **refulgent** would be shining and radiant. _____

   _____

EXERCISE C   On Beauty

Is beauty perceived with the eyes or with the heart? On a separate sheet of paper, write a paragraph in response to this question, using at least three of the vocabulary words.

Vocabulary Power

Lesson 30   Base Words

A base word is an English word to which prefixes or suffixes are added to form a new word. When you encounter an unfamiliar word, check to see if it contains a base word that you know. For example, if you know that *baffle* means "to confuse," you can figure out that *bafflement* means "confusion." Some base words change their spelling slightly when affixes are added. *Despicable* ("hateful"), for example, contains the base word *despise* ("to hate"). Examine the words listed below to see if you recognize any base words.

Word List

accessible	evocative	hemisphere	sluggish
dispassionate	fanaticism	invigorating	voluminous
dramatization	grandeur		

EXERCISE A   Context Clues

Read each sentence below and use context clues to guess the meaning of the boldfaced word. Write your definition; then, write the dictionary definition that best fits the sentence.

1. The northern **hemisphere** is the section of Earth that lies north of the equator.

   My definition _____

   Dictionary definition _____

2. Some issues create such strong feelings that people cannot have **dispassionate** conversations about them.

   My definition _____

   Dictionary definition _____

3. A ramp was added at the front door to make the building **accessible** to people using wheelchairs.

   My definition _____

   Dictionary definition _____

4. The hot weather made me **sluggish** on the soccer field; I seemed to be moving in slow motion as the other players darted past me.

   My definition _____

   Dictionary definition _____

5. The **grandeur** of the "summer cottage," actually a mansion, reflected the immense wealth of the family that owned it.

   My definition _____

   Dictionary definition _____

Vocabulary Power continued

6. After an **invigorating** swim in the chilly Atlantic Ocean, I had plenty of energy to face the rest of my day.

   My definition _____

   Dictionary definition _____

7. It's good to become involved in activities that are important to you, but devotion can become **fanaticism** when a single activity or cause takes over your whole life.

   My definition _____

   Dictionary definition _____

8. This story is strongly **evocative;** the author describes the adventures of a young boy so vividly that I found myself remembering similar experiences from my own childhood.

   My definition _____

   Dictionary definition _____

9. The popular television actress received **voluminous** mail every day from her fans.

   My definition _____

   Dictionary definition _____

10. This play is a **dramatization** of a story by Mark Twain.

    My definition _____

    Dictionary definition _____

EXERCISE B **Multiple-Meaning Words**

Many words in English have more than one meaning. Each meaning, however, is based on the meaning of the word root. The word *voluminous*, for example, is from the Latin root, *volumin-*, meaning "roll" or "scroll." A dictionary entry for *voluminous* lists several different meanings, but all of them are related to the root meanings "roll" or "scroll." On a separate sheet of paper, write the precise definition of *voluminous* as it is used in each sentence below.

1. The labyrinth consisted of **voluminous** twists and turns.

2. Her **voluminous** skirt completely hid the piano stool on which she sat.

3. The office manager tried to organize the **voluminous** late slips.

4. The main library has a superb collection of the **voluminous** writings of the Romantic poets.

Vocabulary Power

Lesson 31   The Greek Root *graph/gram*

As you know, many words in the English language developed from the ancient Greek. Knowing the meanings of Greek roots can help you understand English words. The root *graph,* which is sometimes spelled *gram,* means "to write." Several of the words in this list are derived from *graph/gram.*

Word List

cartography	epigone	epitome	seismograph
epicenter	epigram	graphology	topography
epidermis	epistle		

EXERCISE A Context Clues

Read each sentence below and use context clues to guess the meaning of the boldfaced word. Write your definition. Then, write the dictionary definition that best fits the sentence.

1. Scientists interpreted data from a **seismograph** to determine the strength of the earthquake.

   My definition _____

   Dictionary definition _____

2. Egyptian **cartography** in the fourteenth century B.C. was used to map the borders of a wealthy person's estate because the flooding of the Nile River regularly washed away property markers.

   My definition _____

   Dictionary definition _____

3. I don't know much about **graphology**, but Celia's precise, orderly handwriting does seem to reflect her personality.

   My definition _____

   Dictionary definition _____

4. Before we set out on our biking expedition, we need a map that shows **topography** so we can avoid hills that are too steep.

   My definition _____

   Dictionary definition _____

5. This clever and insightful **epigram** is part of Alexander Pope's "Essay on Man": "On life's vast ocean diversely we sail, / Reason the card, but passion is the gale."

   My definition _____

   Dictionary definition _____

Vocabulary Power *continued*

6. Charles likes to think of himself as Professor Liederman's star pupil, but most people see him as a pathetic **epigone** who tries too hard to imitate his teacher.

My definition _____

Dictionary definition _____

7. Although the **epicenter** of the earthquake was many miles south, the worst damage occurred in the big city, where several buildings collapsed.

My definition _____

Dictionary definition _____

8. Shakespeare's "Sonnet 130" is, for me, the **epitome** of a great love poem.

My definition _____

Dictionary definition _____

9. Although Tori wrote her teacher a lengthy **epistle** explaining why her term paper was three months late, she still failed the course.

My definition _____

Dictionary definition _____

10. Are freckles located in the **epidermis**, or do they simply show through the outer layer of skin?

My definition _____

Dictionary definition _____

EXERCISE B   Word Association
Write the vocabulary word that fits best in each list.

1. postcard, telegram, letter   _____

2. charting, mapping, drawing   _____

3. hair, fingernails, flesh   _____

4. mountains, valleys, rivers   _____

5. example, ideal, type   _____

Vocabulary Power

Lesson 32   Using Reference Skills: Antonyms

Antonyms are words that are opposite or nearly opposite in meaning. For example, *happy* and *sad* are antonyms. Many standardized tests include questions that ask you to recognize antonyms. These exercises will give you practice with various types of questions involving antonyms.

EXERCISE A

Read each sentence and consider how the boldfaced word fits with the meaning of the whole sentence. Then, choose the antonym for the boldfaced word that would change the meaning of the sentence to its opposite. Use a dictionary to help you if necessary.

1. I go to the mall only to make **necessary** purchases.
   a. expensive   b. frivolous   c. fashionable   d. multiple

2. Fred's sister gave him a **copious** serving of mashed potatoes.
   a. measly   b. cold   c. delicious   d. lumpy

3. People moved out of the way as Jen skateboarded **ineptly** down the sidewalk.
   a. quickly   b. awkwardly   c. loudly   d. deftly

4. The **intrepid** police officer lost no time jumping into his car and speeding away.
   a. foolish   b. patient   c. experienced   d. cowardly

EXERCISE B

Circle the word whose meaning is most nearly the *opposite* of the boldfaced word.

1. **cheerful**:   bright   doleful   sloppy | 4. **ethereal**:   intellectual   honest   solid

2. **pernicious**: benevolent injurious   secure | 5. **digress**:   scatter   ingest   focus

3. **innate**:   learned   unexamined   harmful | 6. **avarice**:   kindness   generosity   clarity

EXERCISE C

Choose the letter of the antonym that best completes each analogy.

1. honest : unethical :: animated : _____
   a. lackluster   b. silent   c. ostentatious   d. subtle

2. confidence : trepidation :: acquiescence : _____
   a. acknowledgment   b. defiance   c. confusion   d. excitement

3. uniform : variegated :: apt : _____
   a. silly   b. inappropriate   c. cynical   d. talented

4. glad : distraught :: diligent : _____
   a. single-minded   b. comely   c. lush   d. indolent

5. diverge : merge :: disdain : _____
   a. hold   b. examine   c. admire   d. subside

Vocabulary Power

Review: Unit 8

EXERCISE

Circle the letter of the word that best completes each sentence.

1. Jack stared at the graffiti for a long time, trying to figure it out, but still he found its meaning _____.
   a. erudite   **b.** dispassionate   **c.** evocative   **d.** inscrutable

2. Some people find running early in the morning to be _____, but I feel tired just thinking about it.
   a. ineffable   **b.** invigorating   **c.** sluggish   **d.** intangible

3. Few tourists see the island's most beautiful waterfall because it is _____ only by a narrow footpath that winds treacherously uphill for five miles.
   a. intangible   **b.** accessible   **c.** aesthetic   **d.** voluminous

4. It's amazing how experts in _____ can transfer natural features such as streams, mountains, and coastlines accurately onto a flat piece of paper.
   a. hemisphere   **b.** graphology   **c.** cartography   **d.** edification

5. A mere postcard cannot show the _____ of this mountain range; you must go there and see it yourself.
   a. grandeur   **b.** enigma   **c.** epicenter   **d.** epitome

6. A scraped knee affects only the _____ and is not a serious injury, but that does not make it hurt any less.
   a. criterion   **b.** epigone   **c.** dramatization   **d.** epidermis

7. The main character in this play is a(n) _____; she seems to be in love with her husband, and yet she keeps doing things that hurt him.
   a. epigone   **b.** connoisseur   **c.** enigma   **d.** epistle

8. The _____ in this national park is extremely varied, ranging from wide, flat prairies to soaring mountain ranges to deep-cut canyons.
   a. graphology   **b.** topography   **c.** seismograph   **d.** cartography

9. James is very _____ because he reads three books a week on a wide range of subjects.
   a. refulgent   **b.** ineffable   **c.** accessible   **d.** erudite

10. Paul's _____ to his girlfriend explains the meaning of real love.
    a. epistle   **b.** epigram   **c.** criterion   **d.** dramatization

Vocabulary Power

Test: Unit 8

PART A

Circle the word in parentheses that best completes each sentence.

1. The entire short story was written in the form of a(n) (seismograph, enigma, epistle) from a mother to her son.

2. Our final project in English class was to write and perform a(n) (dramatization, epigram, criterion) of a short story by Nadine Gordimer.

3. Erica's (grandeur, fanaticism, graphology) for politics caused her to quit her job and move to Washington, D.C.

4. In August, when everyone's gardens bear fruit at once, the neighborhood has a(n) (voluminous, evocative, inscrutable) supply of tomatoes, cucumbers, and hot peppers.

5. Filipo is not selective about movies; his only (criterion, connoisseur, epitome) is that a film involve lots of animals.

6. Although the earthquake caused some damage, data from the (topography, hemisphere, seismograph) indicated that the earthquake had not been a particularly strong tremor.

7. Many religious truths are considered to be (resplendent, accessible, ineffable); they cannot be described in words and must, therefore, be directly experienced.

8. Do you think that (cartography, graphology, topography) is a valid way to study a person's character?

9. Rachel is the (epitome, epigram, epicenter) of a well-rounded student: she gets good grades, participates in three sports, is president of the student council, and does community service.

10. It's important that food, water, and the litter box be (erudite, accessible, voluminous) to the cats at all times.

11. A portion of the continent of Africa lies in the northern (epidermis, hemisphere, cartography), but much of it is south of the equator.

12. I was surprised that Monica gave such a(n) (ineffable, invigorating, dispassionate) response to questions about very emotional issues.

13. This painting, strongly (inscrutable, sluggish, evocative) of the English countryside, brought a high price.

14. The (erudite, refulgent, invigorating) ornament glistened near the top of the Christmas tree.

15. Proper role models can contribute to a person's (edification, grandeur, epistle).

Vocabulary Power *continued*

PART B

For each boldfaced word, circle the letter of the word that is most nearly *opposite* in meaning.

1. resplendent
   - **a.** scary
   - **b.** exciting
   - **c.** incoherent
   - **d.** dull

2. inscrutable
   - **a.** noisy
   - **b.** obvious
   - **c.** melodious
   - **d.** solid

3. invigorating
   - **a.** cold
   - **b.** exhausting
   - **c.** educational
   - **d.** illogical

4. sluggish
   - **a.** slender
   - **b.** intelligent
   - **c.** swift
   - **d.** furry

5. grandeur
   - **a.** shabbiness
   - **b.** enormity
   - **c.** obscurity
   - **d.** peace

6. erudite
   - **a.** ignorant
   - **b.** ugly
   - **c.** fashionable
   - **d.** brief

7. voluminous
   - **a.** witty
   - **b.** tiny
   - **c.** sleepy
   - **d.** sharp

8. intangible
   - **a.** overwhelming
   - **b.** important
   - **c.** indescribable
   - **d.** concrete

9. fanaticism
   - **a.** wisdom
   - **b.** talent
   - **c.** moderation
   - **d.** strength

10. epigone
    - **a.** postscript
    - **b.** genius
    - **c.** novel
    - **d.** leader

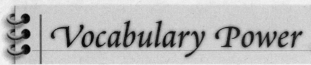

Vocabulary Power

Lesson 33   Using Synonyms

Feelings can be endlessly bewildering, mysterious, and complicated. Even if we never directly feel frantic, elated, or complacent, we can read and learn about those emotions. As the world grows smaller, mutual understanding becomes increasingly important. Thus, the words in this lesson will help you to label and comprehend the emotions you read about as well as the ones you experience.

Word List

despicable	intrepid	ludicrous	ostracize
diffident	languish	magnanimous	regale
dogmatic	levity		

EXERCISE A Synonyms

Each boldfaced vocabulary word below is paired with a synonym whose meaning you probably know. Think of other words related to the meaning of the synonym and write your ideas on the line provided. Then, look up the vocabulary word in a dictionary and write its meaning.

1. **ludicrous:** absurd _____

   Dictionary definition _____

2. **diffident:** shy _____

   Dictionary definition _____

3. **languish:** droop _____

   Dictionary definition _____

4. **ostracize:** banish _____

   Dictionary definition _____

5. **dogmatic:** arrogant _____

   Dictionary definition _____

6. **levity:** frivolity _____

   Dictionary definition _____

7. **magnanimous:** noble _____

   Dictionary definition _____

8. **despicable:** contemptible _____

   Dictionary definition _____

9. **regale:** entertain _____

   Dictionary definition _____

10. **intrepid:** courageous _____

    Dictionary definition _____

Vocabulary Power *continued*

EXERCISE B   Context Clues

Draw a line through the italicized word or phrase. Above it, write the vocabulary word that can replace the word or phrase.

1. The teacher's *characterized by an authoritative point of view put forth without adequate grounds* interpretation of the fairy tale confused many students.

2. All crimes are *deserving to be despised* acts.

3. *Frivolity* in a hospital waiting room may seem out of place, but telling funny stories can help pass the time and cut down on fear and worry.

4. Sally could do nothing but *be weak* at home for weeks after her breakup.

5. The *characterized by fearlessness, fortitude, and endurance* volunteers risked their lives to get medical supplies to the people trapped in the flood zone.

6. They were asking a(n) *laughable due to obvious absurdity* amount of money for their used car.

7. Because of her drug use, her so-called friends began to *exclude from a group* her.

8. Her *reserved* manner made people think she was a snob.

9. The philanthropist's *unselfish* act of sending twenty-five city children to summer camp was on the evening news.

10. Carl always tries to *entertain* us with the same anecdotes at every party.

EXERCISE C   Multiple-Meaning Words

Use a dictionary to find the definition of each of the following multiple-meaning words that relate to ostracism. Then, write a sentence for each word showing how it can be used.

1. scapegoat _____

   Sentence _____

2. exile _____

   Sentence _____

3. excommunicate _____

   Sentence _____

4. expatriate _____

   Sentence _____

5. purge _____

   Sentence _____

Name _____ Date _____ Class _____

Vocabulary Power

Lesson 34   Prefixes Meaning "for" and "against"

When added to roots, the prefixes *counter-, contra-, anti-,* and *pro-* form words with different meanings related to the ideas of favoring or opposing something or someone. Knowing these prefixes will help you to analyze and understand a large number of English words.

Word	Definition
antigravity	the effect of canceling gravity
contraband	goods that are against the law
counterproductive	working against a goal; tending to hinder one's purpose
procrastinate	to delay; to put off intentionally and habitually

Word List

antagonize	contraindicate	countermand	prodigious
antibiotic	contravene	procure	proscribe
anticlimax	counterbalance		

EXERCISE Word Etymologies

Choose the vocabulary word that best matches each clue. Write your own definition of the word and check it against a dictionary definition.

1. This word comes from the Latin *prodigium*, meaning "an unnatural thing." You had better be prepared for someone with this kind of an appetite. _____

   My definition _____

   Dictionary definition _____

2. This word combines the prefix *contra-* and the root *venire*, meaning "to come." If you oppose a community's rule or law, you could do this at a local government meeting. _____

   My definition _____

   Dictionary definition _____

3. The prefix *anti-* and the root word *biōtikos,* meaning "having a (specified) mode of life." This is something that is used to destroy bacterial life. _____

   My definition _____

   Dictionary definition _____

Vocabulary Power *continued*

4. This word combines the prefix *pro-*, meaning "for," and the root word *cura*, meaning "to care." Someone who does this makes a special effort for someone else. _____

   My definition _____

   Dictionary definition _____

5. The prefix *countre-* and the root word *mander*, meaning "to command," combine to form this word. In the army, only an officer of high rank can do this. _____

   My definition _____

   Dictionary definition _____

6. This word is made up of the prefix *anti-* and the root word *agon*, meaning "contest." Doing this will not make you popular. _____

   My definition _____

   Dictionary definition _____

7. The prefix *counter-* and the root word *bilanx*, meaning "having two scalepans," combine to form this word. If you have done something wrong, doing a good deed might do this. _____

   My definition _____

   Dictionary definition _____

8. This word is built from the prefix *pro-* and the root word *scribere*, meaning "to write." If you aren't allowed to stay out late on school nights, someone has done this. _____

   My definition _____

   Dictionary definition _____

9. The prefix *contra-* and the root word *indicare*, meaning "to proclaim," combine to form this word. When this happens, it is not advisable to do something. _____

   My definition _____

   Dictionary definition _____

10. The prefix *anti-* and the Greek root word *klimax*, meaning "ladder," combine to form this word. A movie you really wanted to see may end up being this if it disappoints you. _____

    My definition _____

    Dictionary definition _____

Vocabulary Power

Lesson 35   The Greek Root *bio* and the Latin Root *vit*

The Greek root *bio* comes from the word *bios,* meaning "life." Therefore, *biology* is the study of living things, and a *biography* is an account of a person's life written by another. The Latin root *vit* comes from the word *vita,* meaning "life." Thus, vitamins are organic compounds necessary for maintaining life. This lesson will feature many other words that all relate to life and living.

Word List

amphibian	microbe	viable	vivacious
bionic	revive	vitality	vivid
biopsy	symbiosis		

EXERCISE A   Context Clues

Write the vocabulary word that best matches each clue. Write your own definition of the word and check it against a dictionary definition.

1. This word comes from the Latin word *vivere,* meaning "to live." It is an adjective used to describe someone who loves to celebrate. _____

   My definition _____

   Dictionary definition _____

2. This word comes from the Greek words *ambi,* meaning "both," and *bios,* meaning "life." A frog is an example of this noun. _____

   My definition _____

   Dictionary definition _____

3. This word combines the prefix *re-* and the Latin word *vivere,* meaning "to live." This action might occur in a hospital emergency room. _____

   My definition _____

   Dictionary definition _____

4. This word comes from the prefix *bi-* and the Greek root *opsis*, meaning "appearance." This is a diagnostic process that doctors might use to discover whether a lump is cancerous. _____

   My definition _____

   Dictionary definition _____

5. This adjective comes from the Latin word *vita,* meaning "life." If you were to discover old seeds, you might wonder whether they were still capable of being this. _____

   My definition _____

   Dictionary definition _____

Vocabulary Power *continued*

6. This noun combines the prefix *mikro-*, meaning "small," and the Greek word *bios*, meaning "life." It refers to something that cannot be seen with the naked eye. _____

My definition _____

Dictionary definition _____

7. This noun comes from the Latin word *vitalis*, meaning "of life." Someone who has this is energized and excited. _____

My definition _____

Dictionary definition _____

8. This noun comes from the prefix *sym-*, meaning "together," and the Greek word *bios*, meaning "life." This type of relationship is helpful to two or more animals. _____

My definition _____

Dictionary definition _____

9. This adjective comes from the Latin word *vivere*, meaning "to live." It is an adjective used to describe colors, experience, and the imagination. _____

My definition _____

Dictionary definition _____

10. This word is a blend of the Greek word *bi-* and *-onics*, as in *electronic*. Someone who loses a limb might receive this kind of replacement. _____

My definition _____

Dictionary definition _____

EXERCISE B Usage

If the boldfaced word is correctly used in the sentence, write *correct* above it. If not, draw a line through the word and write in the correct vocabulary word.

1. Novelist Gene Stratton Porter created a **vivacious** portrait of a vast, primitive swamp and its residents in *A Girl of the Limberlost.*

2. Steve Austin of *The Six Million Dollar Man* television show had **bionic** body parts implanted after he crashed an experimental plane.

3. After two weeks, the doctors determined that the patient's skin graft was **vivacious,** and they thought little scarring would occur once the area had healed.

4. As an **amphibian,** the frog grows from a water-breathing tadpole into an air-breathing frog.

5. Cool water and rest **revived** Sonia after she had fainted during the summer band performance.

Vocabulary Power

Lesson 36   Using Test-Taking Skills

Analogies

An analogy is a similarity between things that are otherwise dissimilar. On a test, an analogy gives a pair of words. To answer correctly, you must identify another pair of words that has a relationship similar to the relationship between the words in the given pair. These questions on vocabulary tests and standardized examinations measure your ability to think critically about the relationships between words. These tips will help you complete analogies.

1. Determine the relationship between the given words.
   novel : writer :: **(a)** song : choir   **(b)** symphony : composer   **(c)** law : judge   **(d)** poet : poem
   A novel is created by a writer. The relationship between the two words is that of a product and a producer. Therefore, you must look for the answer that expresses the same or a similar relationship. Here are some examples of other relationships:

Relationship	Example	Relationship	Example
antonyms	aware : unconscious	size	stone : boulder
synonyms	forbid : prohibit	cause/effect	rain : flood
class/member	vehicle : automobile	object/purpose	seat belt : safety

2. Watch for reversed elements in answer choices. In the example above, **(d)** poet : poem is similar to novel : writer, but here the relationship is producer and product.
3. Eliminate the word pairs that have different relationships. Knowing that you are looking for a product/producer relationship, you can eliminate choices **(a)** and **(c)**.
4. Examine all answer choices to make sure that you have selected the best one. The remaining pair, **(b)** symphony : composer, is the correct answer.

EXERCISE

Choose the word pair that best completes the following analogies.

1. active : passive :: _____
   a. stillness : night
   b. innocence : purity
   c. accumulate : riches
   d. diligent : lazy

2. engine : car :: _____
   a. speed : racecar   **b.** heart : organ   **c.** brain : thought   **d.** lightbulb : lamp

3. canine : dog :: _____
   a. bovine : cow   **b.** feline : deer   **c.** tiger : cat   **d.** mammal : elephant

4. conflagration : flame :: _____
   a. hose : water   **b.** fire : ash   **c.** hurricane : breeze   **d.** log : kindling

5. prisoner : escape :: _____
   a. student : daydream
   b. dog : bark
   c. guitar : string
   d. steal : criminal

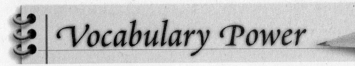

Vocabulary Power

Review: Unit 9

EXERCISE

Circle the letter of the phrase that best explains the boldfaced vocabulary word.

1. You can expect that a **magnanimous** gesture would be performed _____.
   - **a.** out of the goodness of someone's heart
   - **b.** to explain or excuse negative behavior
   - **c.** in order to promote one's own self-interest
   - **d.** to prevent a person from getting cancer

2. When someone **countermands** an order, that person _____.
   - **a.** frees others from a controlling force or influence
   - **b.** interrupts an important connection
   - **c.** cancels or reverses a previous directive
   - **d.** drives a hard bargain

3. If you contemplate **viable** alternatives, you think about _____.
   - **a.** decisions to be made
   - **b.** possibilities that are capable of success or effectiveness
   - **c.** concrete choices that are logically organized
   - **d.** excuses that are similar in position, value, structure, or function

4. If a new acquaintance is **diffident**, he or she will _____.
   - **a.** take some time to feel comfortable in your presence
   - **b.** be warm and outgoing from the very beginning
   - **c.** do things motivated by meanness or lack of generosity
   - **d.** act in advance to deal with any unexpected difficulty

5. If you have a **prodigious** amount of food left after a party, you can expect _____.
   - **a.** to face a situation that causes perplexity
   - **b.** that an angry dispute will follow
   - **c.** to be unable to calculate the quantity
   - **d.** to be eating leftovers for a while

6. **Symbiosis** between a cow and a bird, for example, would mean that they _____.
   - **a.** care nothing about right and wrong
   - **b.** attack each other for environmental purposes
   - **c.** have a relationship of mutual benefit or dependence
   - **d.** attack each other and compete for food

7. A **dogmatic** individual is likely to _____.
   - **a.** listen carefully and objectively to all sides of an issue
   - **b.** disagree with any contrary points of view
   - **c.** be easily influenced by the opinions of others
   - **d.** show a disposition to believe readily and wholeheartedly

8. A child with a **vivid** imagination _____.
   - **a.** is active in forming lifelike images in his or her mind
   - **b.** lacks the ability to discriminate between fantasy and reality
   - **c.** deserves special praise or commendation
   - **d.** is easily confused

Vocabulary Power

Test: Unit 9

PART A

Circle the letter of the word that best completes the sentence.

1. Lorna feels _____ around her tall friends since she is only five feet tall.
   a. dogmatic **b.** magnanimous **c.** diffident **d.** vivid

2. Millie was forced to somehow _____ her friends' desire to have her at college with them with her parents' desire to have her stay home.
   a. counterbalance **b.** contravene **c.** antagonize **d.** procure

3. With the _____ legs that replaced the ones he lost in the accident, the truck driver found he could jump a lot higher than he could before.
   a. despicable **b.** vivid **c.** bionic **d.** viable

4. The doctor had to _____ Hillary's knee surgery because of the possibility of blood clots.
   a. countermand **b.** contraindicate **c.** antagonize **d.** procure

5. A(n) _____ can often be done in the outpatient clinic because the procedure is relatively simple: the doctor merely cuts away some tissue to examine under a microscope.
   a. symbiosis **b.** microbe **c.** amphibian **d.** biopsy

6. The color of Estelle's clothing was so _____ that her hair and makeup seemed overpowered and pale.
   a. vivid **b.** vivacious **c.** magnanimous **d.** despicable

7. No one realized that the "lizard" was actually a(n) _____ until Jim discovered it swimming in a bucket of water one morning.
   a. biopsy **b.** microbe **c.** amphibian **d.** levity

8. In one type of _____, a marine worm that lives in hermit crab shells comes out of the shell to share the hermit crab's food.
   a. symbiosis **b.** vitality **c.** levity **d.** antibiotic

9. Some storytellers will _____ you with silly anecdotes while others will tell compelling tales.
   a. countermand **b.** regale **c.** ostracize **d.** languish

10. Diane was such a poorly organized manager that she frequently got confused and would _____ her own instructions to her team.
    a. regale **b.** contravene **c.** countermand **d.** ostracize

11. Alita was truly _____ when she invited Debbie to her graduation party, especially considering that Debbie had stolen her boyfriend.
    a. viable **b.** despicable **c.** magnanimous **d.** diffident

Vocabulary Power continued

12. Donald would _____ any dog he saw behind a fence until one bit him.
   a. counterbalance   **b.** antagonize   **c.** ostracize   **d.** languish

13. Cacti are the most _____ plants for drought conditions.
   a. viable   **b.** vivacious   **c.** bionic   **d.** ludicrous

14. Tom holds very _____ views on politics; he agrees with all of the views promoted by his church.
   a. dogmatic   **b.** ludicrous   **c.** prodigious   **d.** intrepid

15. The actor's tragic death in his own swimming pool was a sad _____ to a short and promising career.
   a. antibiotic   **b.** vitality   **c.** symbiosis   **d.** anticlimax

PART B

Circle the letter of the word that means most nearly the same as the vocabulary word.

1. revive
   a. blush   **b.** brag   **c.** clarify   **d.** restore

2. proscribe
   a. conduct   **b.** prohibit   **c.** allow   **d.** permit

3. ludicrous
   a. absurd   **b.** superior   **c.** stylish   **d.** strong

4. intrepid
   a. bold   **b.** energetic   **c.** opaque   **d.** irrelevant

5. contravene
   a. assemble   **b.** condemn   **c.** deny   **d.** intersect

6. vitality
   a. defiance   **b.** energy   **c.** authority   **d.** description

7. languish
   a. await   **b.** undermine   **c.** preserve   **d.** droop

8. despicable
   a. loathsome   **b.** admirable   **c.** uncertain   **d.** comfortable

9. microbe
   a. disease   **b.** diagnosis   **c.** germ   **d.** cell

10. ostracize
   a. gossip   **b.** exclude   **c.** warn   **d.** cooperate

Vocabulary Power

Lesson 37   Word Definitions

Whether it is a dramatic event or a typical situation, some experiences make stronger impressions than others. Whether your memory of the occasion lingers or fades depends in large part on who was involved, where it took place, and how it affected you. The words in this lesson will help you to revisit your impressions as well as to comment on them.

Word List

estrange	fiasco	impel	inimitable
extol	foray	impetus	unsavory
farce	gauche		

EXERCISE A   Word Definitions

Circle the letter of the correct definition of the boldfaced vocabulary word.

1. Ellen grew embarrassed as her boss continued to **extol** her work in front of the other employees.

   a. supplement with great effort

   b. praise highly

   c. put to use

   d. compete with successfully

2. Every prima ballerina in a major company has her own **inimitable** style and her own interpretations of the steps.

   a. defying imitation

   b. arousing the emotions

   c. costly

   d. clearly expressed

3. Even for charitable purposes, calling a dinner of greasy chicken and cold french fries a "banquet" was a **farce.**

   a. imitation of the sensible world

   b. playful trick

   c. an essential quality needed for success

   d. absurd pretense

4. Curiosity and a genuine desire to cure disease **impel** research scientists to take on the impossible.

   a. drive forward

   b. punch or strike

   c. suspend an action temporarily

   d. to be at ease or peace

5. Whereas smacking one's lips and belching are ways to show appreciation for food in some cultures, these behaviors are considered **gauche** in the United States.

   a. unpopular

   b. set or keep apart

   c. lacking social polish

   d. cause to swerve from a course

6. An innocent squirrel charging through the area turned the children's dog show into a **fiasco.**

   a. source of something

   b. sudden flood

   c. whirling motion

   d. complete failure

𝒱ocabulary Power *continued*

7. The **unsavory** smells from the restaurant quickly persuaded us to go elsewhere.

   a. zesty

   b. distasteful

   c. having one or more projecting sharp points

   d. marked by violent reactions

8. Mean-spirited gossip can sometimes **estrange** people who have been friends for years.

   a. leave in a helpless position

   b. alienate

   c. arrange in a compact way

   d. bring under control

9. Dimitri made a **foray** into the woods to gather mushrooms.

   a. alternative pattern

   b. secret exchange

   c. symbolic representation

   d. initial attempt outside the usual area

10. Greed was the **impetus** behind the Gold Rush of 1849 in California.

   a. distant object

   b. stimulus

   c. something difficult to classify

   d. arguable premise

EXERCISE B   Synonyms

Circle the letter of the word that means most nearly the same as the vocabulary word.

1. fiasco

   a. attachment   **b.** failure   **c.** confusion   **d.** cruelty

2. foray

   a. adventure   **b.** raid   **c.** delay   **d.** demand

3. farce

   a. discoloration   **b.** discipline   **c.** elegance   **d.** mockery

4. extol

   a. praise   **b.** blame   **c.** enrage   **d.** enlarge

5. impel

   a. cringe   **b.** perpetuate   **c.** injure   **d.** urge

6. impetus

   a. circulation   **b.** disciple   **c.** turbulence   **d.** impulse

EXERCISE C   Multiple-Meaning Words

One of the words in this lesson, *gauche*, and its antonym, *adroit*, come from French. Using a dictionary or an encyclopedia of word origins, research the history of these words. Then, on a separate sheet of paper, write a brief paragraph about how the derivations relate to the current meaning. Are there any differences or similarities between the current and original meanings? Do these two words have more than one meaning?

Vocabulary Power

Lesson 38   The Greek Roots *phos* and *phot* and the Latin Root *luc*

Greek and Latin have given us a number of words related to the subject of light. The Greek roots *phos* and *phot* mean "light," while the Latin root *luc* comes from the word *lucere*, meaning "to shine." *Phosphene* is the sensation of light you get behind your eyelids when you press on them, and something that is *pellucid* admits the passage of light. All the words in this lesson share a common meaning.

Word List

elucidate	lucubration	photograph	photosynthesis
lucent	phosphorescent	photosensitive	translucent
lucid	photogenic		

EXERCISE A   Clues Matching

Choose the vocabulary word that best matches each clue. On the lines provided, write your own definition of the word and check it against the dictionary definition.

1. This word comes from three Greek words: *photo*, *syn*, meaning "together with," and *tithenai*, meaning "to put." It refers to a process used by green plants. _____

   My definition _____

   Dictionary definition _____

2. This adjective comes from the Latin word *lucere*, meaning "to shine." Doctors might ask you several questions to make sure you are this following a head injury. _____

   My definition _____

   Dictionary definition _____

3. This adjective from the Greek root *phos* is used to describe glow-in-the-dark toys. _____

   My definition _____

   Dictionary definition _____

4. This verb comes from the Latin word *lucidus*, meaning "bright." It is something that you would expect knowledgeable people to do if you questioned them. _____

   My definition _____

   Dictionary definition _____

5. This word comes from the Greek root *phot*. It may describe photographic paper or a person's eyes. _____

   My definition _____

   Dictionary definition _____

Vocabulary Power *continued*

6. This noun comes from the Latin word *lucubrare*, meaning "to work by lamplight." A scholar might be involved in this. _____

   My definition _____

   Dictionary definition _____

7. This word comes from the Greek root *phot*. Certain camera subjects are this. _____

   My definition _____

   Dictionary definition _____

8. This adjective from the Latin prefix *trans-*, meaning "through," and the word *lucere*, is typically used to describe a window. _____

   My definition _____

   Dictionary definition _____

9. This noun from the Greek word *phot* refers to a memento of people and places. _____

   My definition _____

   Dictionary definition _____

10. This adjective comes from the Latin word *lucere*. A house with lighted windows could be described as this. _____

    My definition _____

    Dictionary definition _____

EXERCISE B **Researching Etymologies**

Many other words in the English language, especially new scientific terms, use the Greek roots *phos* and *phot*. Choose one of these words, research it, and write a brief report, relating your explanation to the root meaning of "light." Here are some words to consider: *photon, phosphate, phosphorus, photic, photocoagulation, photoplay, photo essay*, or *photokinesis*. Write your report on a separate sheet of paper.

Vocabulary Power

Lesson 39   The Latin Root *memor* and Prefix *retro-*

The Latin root *memor*, meaning "mindful," and the Latin prefix *retro-*, meaning "backward" or "back," are the sources of English words that express past ideas. For example, something that is *memorable* is worth being remembered. If you consider something in *retrospect*, you are looking backward or reviewing the past. The words in this lesson will help you talk about experiences that occurred at an earlier time.

Word List

commemorate	memorabilia	retrofit	retrogress
immemorial	memorandum	retrograde	retrospective
memoir	retroactive		

EXERCISE A   Clues Matching

Supply the vocabulary word that best matches each clue. Then, write your own definition and check it against the dictionary definition.

1. This word from the prefix *retro-* and the Latin word *specere*, meaning "to look," can apply to an artist's work about the past. _____

   My definition _____

   Dictionary definition _____

2. This noun comes from the Latin word *memoria*, meaning "memory." You might read this to discover the secrets of your favorite author. _____

   My definition _____

   Dictionary definition _____

3. This word combines the prefix *retro-* and the Latin word *gradi*, meaning "to go." The economy might do this after several months of expansion. _____

   My definition _____

   Dictionary definition _____

4. This word comes from the Latin word *memorabilis*, meaning "memorable." Collectors sometimes pay high prices for this material. _____

   My definition _____

   Dictionary definition _____

5. The prefix *retro-* added to the Latin word *agere*, meaning "to drive," produces this word that might apply to a pay increase that begins in September but applies back to July. _____

   My definition _____

   Dictionary definition _____

Vocabulary Power *continued*

6. This word is created when the prefix *com-*, meaning "with," is added to the word *memor*, meaning "mindful." You might buy a stamp that does this for a movie star. _____

My definition _____

Dictionary definition _____

7. This word combines the prefix *retro-* with the Old English word *fitt*, meaning "strife." People who have purchased cars before airbags were available would have to do this to get airbags. _____

My definition _____

Dictionary definition _____

8. This word comes from the Latin word *memorandus*, meaning "to remind." This is a method of communicating in a business environment. _____

My definition _____

Dictionary definition _____

9. This word comes from the prefix *im-*, meaning "not," and the Latin word *memorialis*, meaning "memory." This word refers to a time before written or oral records. _____

My definition _____

Dictionary definition _____

10. This word is built from the prefix *retro-* and the Latin word *gradi*, meaning "to go." This apparent phenomenon in planets' movements is due to different rates of orbital speed. _____

My definition _____

Dictionary definition _____

EXERCISE B **Technology and Memory**

Given the advanced state of technology today, how might you preserve an experience so that you do not have to rely on memory? On a separate sheet of paper, write an explanation of the kind of technology you would use, how you would apply it, and when you would be most likely to use it. In your explanation, use at least five of the vocabulary words from this lesson.

Name _____ Date _____ Class _____

 # Vocabulary Power

Lesson 40   Using Test-Taking Skills
Sentence Completion

Sentence-completion questions, often included in the verbal portion of standardized tests, call upon your knowledge of vocabulary as well as your critical-thinking skills. In these items, you are required to supply a missing word or words that fit into the context of the sentence. To do so, you must understand the ideas in the sentence. These tips will help you determine meaning from context so that you can better answer sentence-completion questions.

1. Read the entire sentence, noting where the missing word or words are.
2. Analyze the structure of the sentence, searching the context for clues to the overall meaning. A sentence may offer reasons or examples, present a contrast, or give a definition. In this sample sentence, a close synonym provides the needed clue.
   The theme of the novel concerns the _____ of perpetuating a meaningless feud from generation to generation.
   (a) foresight   (b) force   (c) fortitude   (d) folly
3. Eliminate the incorrect answer choices. *Foresight* and *force* make no sense because they have more positive connotations than the rest of the sentence contains. "Strength of mind," part of the definition of *fortitude,* also does not make sense in this context.
4. Substitute the remaining answer choice or choices. In this case, *folly* and *perpetuating a meaningless feud through generations* work together effectively.

EXERCISE

Circle the letter of the word or pair of words that best completes each of the following sentences.

1. Carolyn displays _____ by writing a paragraph when a sentence would be sufficient.
   a. brevity   **b.** verbosity   **c.** animosity   **d.** intolerance

2. To avoid having to repeat the announcement, Mr. Coelho waited until everyone was _____ before speaking.
   a. assembled   **b.** forged   **c.** cloistered   **d.** swarmed

3. A new group of volunteers _____ the weary group that had been stacking sandbags in an effort to _____ the flood waters.
   a. rebuked, placate   **c.** replaced, halt
   b. depressed, preserve   **d.** admired, avoid

4. Millions of voters _____ guerrilla threats to _____ the country's first presidential election.
   a. forgot, win   **c.** made, cancel
   b. defied, participate in   **d.** heard, defeat

5. Scientists _____ that Antarctica, now _____ and covered with ice, was once temperate and filled with plant life.
   a. demand, distant   **b.** insist, withered   **c.** believe, barren   **d.** warn, subdued

6. Sheila finds it easy to _____ the behavior her friends expect since they share similar values.
   a. conform to   **b.** force   **c.** pretend about   **d.** substitute

Vocabulary Power

Review: Unit 10
EXERCISE

Circle the letter of the phrase that best explains the boldfaced vocabulary word.

1. If your party turned into a **fiasco**, people will remember it as _____.
   a. an occasion poorly suited to a particular function or situation
   b. a complete failure
   c. an indication of the existence of something
   d. a mistake in timing

2. Someone who is **photogenic** might be well suited to a career as a _____.
   a. model   b. medical technician   c. camera repair person   d. research biologist

3. If you want to **commemorate** a particular event, your goal is to _____.
   a. obtain money or benefits from it in order to achieve personal gain
   b. attack, damage, or otherwise destroy it by underhanded means
   c. preside over a meeting about it
   d. conduct a ceremony to honor the occasion

4. If someone admits to having the **impetus** to do something, he or she is acknowledging a(n) _____.
   a. stimulus or impelling force   c. sense of amusement
   b. wild or turbulent disturbance   d. feeling of romance

5. When asked to **elucidate** a comment, you would _____.
   a. divide it into sections   c. make it clear by explanation
   b. smile in a silly, self-conscious way d. create a model of it

6. If your approach to a subject is **retrospective**, it is _____.
   a. free from showiness or ostentation   c. very unpleasant or annoying
   b. directed toward the past   d. greater than others in importance or rank

7. One way to **estrange** yourself from a friend would be to _____.
   a. misunderstand something they say to you   c. progress by moving steadily into dating
   b. follow a crowd to a concert   d. move away and never contact them again

8. A **lucid** news report would be one that is _____.
   a. clear and easily understood   c. producing positive results
   b. heedless of danger   d. recurring with measured regularity

9. A **memorandum** is written to _____.
   a. criticize the efforts of a colleague c. remind others of something important
   b. curtail inappropriate behavior   d. question authority

10. An **inimitable** style might be described as _____.
    a. indifferent to criticism   b. unparalleled   c. ill-humored   d. recklessly daring

Vocabulary Power

Test: Unit 10

Circle the letter of the word that best completes the sentence.

1. Alan was hoping that if he just waited long enough, he could _____ his power saw with a laser that could cut down branches from a distance.
   a. retrogress   **b.** commemorate   **c.** photograph   **d.** retrofit

2. Small children who are enchanted by the _____ gleam of fireflies catch them so they can glow in a glass jar.
   a. photosensitive   **b.** phosphorescent   **c.** translucent   **d.** unsavory

3. After her first brave _____ into the garden, Miranda the cat was content to stay inside and watch the moths.
   a. foray   **b.** farce   **c.** lucubration   **d.** retrospective

4. Following cataract surgery, some patients must wear sunglasses even indoors because their eyes are extremely _____.
   a. photogenic   **b.** photosensitive   **c.** retroactive   **d.** gauche

5. Mel can travel to Italy this spring after all since his pay raise, which begins in May, is _____ to January 1.
   a. lucent   **b.** inimitable   **c.** retroactive   **d.** immemorial

6. Rob will probably never be a best-selling author because his fiction is the product of _____ and empty intellectualization.
   a. lucubration   **b.** photosynthesis   **c.** retrospective   **d.** memorabilia

7. Annie Dillard's books are a _____ of her years growing up in Pittsburgh and of the city's natural history.
   a. memorandum   **b.** memorabilia   **c.** memoir   **d.** foray

8. Alicia is so _____ that her father jokes about her having a personal relationship with the camera.
   a. phosphorescent   **b.** gauche   **c.** immemorial   **d.** photogenic

9. Once daffodils and tulips lose their blossoms, some people remove the plants from their garden; however, this prevents _____, and the plants cannot bloom again the next year.
   a. impetus   **b.** photosynthesis   **c.** retrospective   **d.** farce

10. When Ben went to college, his mother cleaned out boxes of baseball cards, postcards, and matchbook covers from the attic, never realizing that this _____ could someday be very valuable.
    a. memoir   **b.** memorabilia   **c.** foray   **d.** retrospective

11. "You haven't been home for a meal since time _____," Mrs. Durston said sarcastically to her teenaged children.
    a. immemorial   **b.** translucent   **c.** phosphorescent   **d.** unsavory

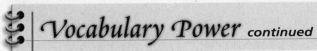

Vocabulary Power continued

12. The homeroom captain will _____ the rule changes students should know by the end of the first week of school.
   a. retrofit   **b.** commemorate   **c.** elucidate   **d.** extol

13. In the Georgia O'Keeffe _____ at the museum, we saw early paintings quite unlike her familiar style.
   a. retroactive   **b.** retrospective   **c.** farce   **d.** fiasco

14. _____ blue panels of fabric floated over the silhouette of the long green dress, making the young woman look as if she had just stepped out of the sea.
   a. Photogenic   **b.** Gauche   **c.** Inimitable   **d.** Translucent

15. The _____ sent by the assistant manager was also a criticism of the employees who put their weekends before their jobs.
   a. memorandum   **b.** lucubration   **c.** photograph   **d.** photosynthesis

PART B
Circle the letter of the word that means most nearly the same as the boldfaced vocabulary word.

1. retrograde
   a. apparent   **b.** erratic   **c.** genuine   **d.** reversed

2. commemorate
   a. honor   **b.** acquire   **c.** overwhelm   **d.** duplicate

3. lucid
   a. eager   **b.** intelligible   **c.** bold   **d.** industrious

4. farce
   a. drama   **b.** genius   **c.** mockery   **d.** lesson

5. gauche
   a. accomplished   **b.** tactless   **c.** tolerant   **d.** right

6. impetus
   a. renewal   **b.** complaint   **c.** disciple   **d.** stimulus

7. photograph
   a. image   **b.** color   **c.** raid   **d.** tradition

8. lucent
   a. fragile   **b.** common   **c.** luminous   **d.** plain

9. impel
   a. conduct   **b.** propel   **c.** excuse   **d.** ridicule

10. retrogress
   a. decline   **b.** improve   **c.** amend   **d.** retire

Vocabulary Power

Lesson 41 Using Context Clues

In today's world, science and technology play increasingly important roles. Empirical evidence encourages us to define reality as rooted in reason. Within this context, imagination, or the inner ordering of the mind, is often downplayed and even dismissed. Modern thinking sometimes rejects the interplay of imagination, fantasy, and illusion. However, reality is not only outer and objective, nor is it solely inner and subjective. It is a blend of both, an artful balance between inner and outer experience. The words in this lesson provide a seedbed for discussion about these two experiences that converge in a rich and fertile view of human experience.

Word List

annihilate	conspiratorial	diverge	prosaic
audacious	converge	illumination	thwart
conciliatory	derisive		

EXERCISE A **Context Clues**

Write the vocabulary word that best matches each clue below.

1. If you participate in a plan to overthrow the government, you can be accused of this kind of thinking.

   _____

2. The beginning snowboarder may be called this to try such a steep slope right away. _____

3. Three or more roads do this in traffic circles, found frequently in New Jersey and Massachusetts.

   _____

4. This verb can be used to describe what an earthquake can do to buildings in an unprepared city.

   _____

5. You might show your lack of respect for a person by giving this kind of laugh. _____

6. A book or movie like this would probably not hold your interest. _____

7. This happens when you turn on the lights in a dark room. _____

8. The mediator's actions were described this way when she brought opposing sides together to solve their differences. _____

9. This happens when two roads that are parallel turn in different directions. _____

10. Angry citizens did this to the mayor's plans to raise taxes. _____

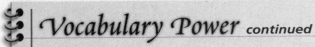

Vocabulary Power *continued*

EXERCISE B Usage
Circle the correct word in parentheses that can be used to complete the sentence.

1. Two roads that (diverge, annihilate, converge) in a wood represent Robert Frost's metaphor for the choice of a life direction.

2. The thunderstorm didn't (converge, conciliate, thwart) our plans for a trip to the zoo.

3. The (conspiratorial, audacious, derisive) thief just walked out the front door with his loot.

4. Angela tried to use a (conspiratorial, conciliatory, prosaic) tone of voice to get the cooperation of both of her relatives.

5. Peanut-butter-and-jelly sandwiches, along with cheese and crackers, comprised a (prosaic, derisive, conspiratorial) menu at the elegant art opening.

6. We decided to use chemicals against the aphids, white flies, and spider mites that threatened to (converge, diverge, annihilate) every plant in the garden.

7. With a loud stage whisper and a(n) (audacious, conspiratorial, derisive) wink, the narrator of the play invited the children to join him in booing the villain.

8. Social, political, and economic factors can (diverge, annihilate, converge) to create a revolutionary movement.

9. Candles provided the only (annihilation, convergence, illumination) for the romantic dinner.

10. With hands on hips and a (derisive, prosaic, conciliatory) smile, Monica taunted, "I told you so."

EXERCISE C Synonyms and Antonyms
Decide which word has the meaning that is the same as (a synonym) or opposite to (an antonym) that of the vocabulary word. Write the letter of your choice on the answer line.

_____ 1. **converge** (synonym)
   a. witness   **b.** cheapen   **c.** meet   **d.** climb

_____ 2. **thwart** (antonym)
   a. encourage   **b.** audit   **c.** leave   **d.** inflame

_____ 3. **annihilate** (synonym)
   a. label   **b.** compound   **c.** straddle   **d.** destroy

_____ 4. **conciliatory** (antonym)
   a. public   **b.** clean   **c.** sleek   **d.** disagreeable

_____ 5. **diverge** (synonym)
   a. chase   **b.** deviate   **c.** minimize   **d.** launch

_____ 6. **prosaic** (antonym)
   a. inventive   **b.** compatible   **c.** deliberate   **d.** reliable

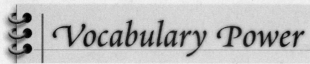

Vocabulary Power

Lesson 42   Using Synonyms

Imagination is the process whereby we convert our perceptions of reality into deep inner meanings unique to us. Along with fantasy, fancy, and illusion, imagination can make a powerful impact on the way we perceive the universe. Our use of illusion can add magic and creativity to a routine assignment. Hand in hand with reason, the various faces of imagination can enhance our view of experience. The words in this lesson can help you to explore and understand the relationship between imagination and your own perceptions of reality.

Word List

curt	fatuous	impinge	privation
depreciate	hinder	parry	ravage
exotic	ignoble		

EXERCISE A Synonyms

Each boldfaced vocabulary word below is paired with a synonym whose meaning you probably know. Think of other words related to the synonym and write them on the line provided. Then, look up the vocabulary word in a dictionary and write its meaning.

1. **fatuous:** foolish _____

   Dictionary definition _____

2. **ravage:** devastate _____

   Dictionary definition _____

3. **curt:** abrupt _____

   Dictionary definition _____

4. **hinder:** obstruct _____

   Dictionary definition _____

5. **depreciate:** reduce _____

   Dictionary definition _____

6. **impinge:** encroach _____

   Dictionary definition _____

7. **exotic:** alien _____

   Dictionary definition _____

8. **privation:** destitution _____

   Dictionary definition _____

9. **ignoble:** sordid _____

   Dictionary definition _____

Vocabulary Power continued

10. parry: deflect _____

Dictionary definition _____

EXERCISE B Usage

If the boldfaced word is used correctly in the sentence, write *correct* above it. If not, draw a line through it and write the correct vocabulary word above it.

1. When the Killiams enclosed their vegetable garden, they didn't realize that the fence would **impinge** on the property next door.

2. When Abner was nervous or upset, he tended to be **curt**, making silly faces, animal noises, and dumb remarks.

3. After the hurricane had destroyed their home, the Ruggiero family faced **privation** and an uncertain future.

4. In today's volatile stock market, company stock values can **ravage** so quickly that short-term investors may be forced to sell at a loss.

5. Severe thunderstorms threatened to **hinder** the landscape for miles.

6. Plants such as orchids, African mallows, and clivias were once viewed as **exotic**, but today they are common.

7. An incoming storm began to **depreciate** the deep-sea salvage operation.

8. **Ignoble** and selfish, Benton was more interested in his fiancée's bank account than in her.

9. The politician tried to **parry** embarrassing questions about office finances.

10. The governor's press secretary cut off the barrage of questions with a **curt** "No comment."

EXERCISE C Word Roots

***Parry*, one of the words in this lesson, comes originally from the sport of fencing, where the word refers to a defensive move in which the fencer deflects or wards off a thrust from an opponent. Many other words from sports have enriched the English language. Research one of the following words in an encyclopedia of word origins or another resource. Then, on a separate sheet of paper, write a brief report about the word, explaining its history, original definition, and current meaning and usage.**

1. **haggard** (falconry)

2. **allure** (falconry)

3. **full tilt** (jousting)

4. **bandy** (tennis)

5. **sidestep** (boxing)

6. **fluke** (billiards)

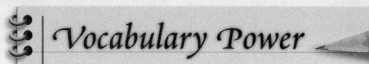

Vocabulary Power

Lesson 43   The Latin Root *ludus*

This lesson has its basis in the Latin infinitive *ludere*, meaning "to play." You can best see how this root operates in the word *illusionist*, a magician or ventriloquist. Illusionists play with reality, convincing us that we are seeing something that is really not there. In this lesson, you will examine how other prefixes combine with variants of the word root to produce a range of words whose meaning is based on play.

Word List

allude	disillusion	illusive	ludicrous
collusion	elude	interlude	preclude
delude	illusionist		

EXERCISE A   Context Clues

Choose the word from the word list that best matches each clue. On the line provided, write your own definition of the word; then, check the definition in a dictionary.

1. This verb is built from *ludere* and the prefix *ex-*, meaning "out of," or "from." A thief could be trying to do this to the police by leaping from one rooftop to another. _____

   My definition _____

   Dictionary definition _____

2. This adjective comes from *ludus*, meaning "play" or "sport." Some soap operas can be described this way; people rarely live such dramatic lives. _____

   My definition _____

   Dictionary definition _____

3. This noun comes from the prefix *com-*, meaning "together," and *ludere*. Groups of people secretly trying to defraud the IRS of money would be involved in this. _____

   My definition _____

   Dictionary definition _____

4. This word from the prefix *inter-*, meaning "between," and *ludus* names a theatrical pause. _____

   My definition _____

   Dictionary definition _____

5. This word comes from the prefixes *dis-* and *in-*, which mean "deprive of" and "not," respectively, and *ludere*. Someone might do this to you by explaining how a magician does a trick. _____

   My definition _____

   Dictionary definition _____

Vocabulary Power continued

6. This verb comes from the prefix *pre-*, meaning "before," and the Latin word *claudere*, "to close." If you do this, you make sure that someone cannot play. _____

My definition _____

Dictionary definition _____

7. This adjective from the Latin prefix *il-* and *ludere* describes some experience. _____

My definition _____

Dictionary definition _____

8. This verb from the prefix *de-*, meaning "remove from," and *ludere,* means "to mislead." _____

My definition _____

Dictionary definition _____

9. This verb combines the prefix *ad-*, meaning "to or toward," with *ludere*. This means to make an indirect reference. _____

My definition _____

Dictionary definition _____

10. This noun, combining the prefix *il-* with *ludere*, refers to a person who performs magic tricks.

_____

My definition _____

Dictionary definition _____

EXERCISE B Multiple-Meaning Words

Many words in English have more than one meaning, all based, however, on the meaning of the word root. The word *chorus*, for example, is from the Greek root *choros*, meaning "ring dance" or "chorus." All of the definitions of *chorus* are related to the root meaning. On a seperate sheet of paper, write the precise dictionary definition of *chorus* as it is used in each sentence below.

1. In ancient Greece, the singers and dancers who performed at religious festivals were known as the **chorus**.

2. In Elizabethan drama, the role of the **chorus** was performed by one actor.

3. In an operatic performance, the **chorus** sings certain parts of works.

4. The dancers and singers supporting the featured players in a musical are known as the **chorus**.

5. The tourists shivered when they heard the mournful **chorus** of howling wolves.

6. Everyone joined in the **chorus** of the Christmas song.

Vocabulary Power

Review: Unit 11

EXERCISE

Write the letter of the phrase that best explains the boldfaced vocabulary word.

1. An extreme sports enthusiast's **audacious** acts might be characterized by his or her _____.

   a. simultaneous nature   **c.** expensive nature

   b. fearless, often reckless, nature   **d.** relationship to certain unorthodox beliefs

2. If someone **impinges** on your privacy, that person _____.

   a. encroaches or trespasses on your territory   **c.** habitually fails to do the right thing

   b. alters it for his or her own purposes   **d.** forms an image of it in his or her own mind

3. If your coach **precludes** the possibility of defeat, he or she _____.

   a. is likely to be fired

   b. introduces negative ideas into the minds of the players

   c. takes the first step toward losing

   d. prevents that condition from taking place

4. Unlike something bold, original, and new, a **prosaic** undertaking is _____.

   a. deserving of disgrace or shame

   b. done with a disguised or concealed identity

   c. dull and commonplace

   d. suitable for those who have achieved their full growth

5. You can logically believe that an **exotic** addition to your life would be _____.

   a. intriguingly unusual   **c.** characterized by romantic imagery

   b. having great emotional impact   **d.** connected to the matter at hand

6. When someone **alludes** to a piece of literature, he or she _____.

   a. takes a keen or zestful pleasure in it

   b. is suggesting something indirectly about the plot, characters, setting, or theme

   c. exposes it to criticism and ridicule

   d. removes it or sets it apart

7. If a design has lines that **converge,** it has thin, threadlike marks that _____.

   a. pass again in the opposite direction

   b. come together at a point

   c. advance in an easy manner

   d. withstand a definite force

Vocabulary Power

Test: Unit 11

PART A

Circle the letter of the word that best completes the sentence.

1. The twins were engaged in a(n) _____ conversation punctuated with giggles and whispers, but they swore they were up to no mischief.
   a. illusive **b.** ignoble **c.** prosaic **d.** conspiratorial

2. A new car starts to _____ as you drive it away from the dealership.
   a. annihilate **b.** ravage **c.** depreciate **d.** converge

3. Not wanting to _____ her coworkers, Jackie hid her previous history as an addict.
   a. disillusion **b.** allude **c.** diverge **d.** thwart

4. Libby was looking forward to a week in the _____ environment of Sandusky, Ohio, after a month of climbing mountains in Nepal.
   a. exotic **b.** prosaic **c.** derisive **d.** curt

5. "Stealing money from the church collection box had to be the work of a(n) _____ scoundrel," the Reverend George Jeeves was heard to say.
   a. ignoble **b.** illusive **c.** ludicrous **d.** derisive

6. The Panthers knew they had to _____ the Dolphins in the last game of the season in order to get into the playoffs.
   a. elude **b.** converge **c.** annihilate **d.** preclude

7. It was a year of _____ for both farmers and migrant workers: drought dried out the vegetable fields; then insects swarmed over the desiccated land.
   a. collusion **b.** interlude **c.** illumination **d.** privation

8. Every time Nance tried to _____ to *Zuleika Dobson* by satirist Max Beerbohm, her friends groaned in boredom and frustration.
   a. delude **b.** allude **c.** depreciate **d.** hinder

9. The rule is that no _____ comments or laughter will be allowed during the presentations since everyone has worked hard and deserves to be taken seriously.
   a. derisive **b.** prosaic **c.** audacious **d.** curt

10. At thirty-five, Keisha decided not to _____ herself anymore—she could no longer become an Olympic gymnast.
    a. allude **b.** preclude **c.** delude **d.** diverge

Vocabulary Power *continued*

11. American cuisine has become more _____ with the addition of Asian and Latin American fruits and vegetables.

    a. fatuous   **b.** ignoble   **c.** exotic   **d.** illusive

12. Leonard chose to spend the _____ between his two interviews in the park, reflecting on his responses.

    a. interlude   **b.** privation   **c.** illumination   **d.** illusionist

13. David depended on excellent vision and the moon's _____ to follow the trail.

    a. illusionist   **b.** interlude   **c.** collusion   **d.** illumination

14. My favorite _____, Harry Houdini, escaped from seemingly impossible situations in his act.

    a. interlude   **b.** illusionist   **c.** illumination   **d.** privation

15. The farmers panicked as the locusts descended to _____ their crops.

    a. hinder   **b.** depreciate   **c.** ravage   **d.** preclude

PART B

Circle the letter of the word that means most nearly the same as the boldfaced word.

1. **diverge**

    a. deviate   **b.** impress   **c.** acquaint   **d.** withdraw

2. **impinge**

    a. abandon   **b.** design   **c.** subdue   **d.** trespass

3. **collusion**

    a. inquiry   **b.** conspiracy   **c.** deduction   **d.** resentment

4. **conciliatory**

    a. looped   **b.** sanctimonious   **c.** ridiculous   **d.** pacifist

5. **curt**

    a. terse   **b.** wordy   **c.** deplorable   **d.** repulsive

6. **illusive**

    a. abundant   **b.** engaging   **c.** deceptive   **d.** oblivious

7. **thwart**

    a. neglect   **b.** obstruct   **c.** encounter   **d.** alleviate

8. **parry**

    a. label   **b.** inflame   **c.** enlighten   **d.** deflect

9. **ludicrous**

    a. absurd   **b.** unseemly   **c.** inevitable   **d.** insensitive

10. **converge**

    a. degrade   **b.** differentiate   **c.** meet   **d.** demolish

Vocabulary Power

Lesson 44   Word Usage

Modern life has been characterized as more hectic, more confused, and more intimidating than any preceding age. While this might be true of our time, people in other times also felt their lives were hectic and confused. About 150 years ago in "The Scholar Gypsy," English poet Matthew Arnold described his age as a "strange disease," characterized by "sick hurry" and "divided aims." The words in this lesson will help you gain a perspective on modern life, with all its excitement, opportunity, and uncertainty.

Word List

callousness	ennui	maudlin	temerity
commiseration	garish	pillage	vehement
denigration	incite		

EXERCISE A   Synonyms

Each boldfaced vocabulary word below is paired with a synonym whose meaning you probably know. Think of other words related to the synonym and write them on the line provided. Then, look up the word in a dictionary and write its meaning.

1. **vehement** : intense _____

   Dictionary definition _____

2. **callousness** : insensitivity _____

   Dictionary definition _____

3. **pillage** : loot _____

   Dictionary definition _____

4. **denigration** : strong criticism _____

   Dictionary definition _____

5. **maudlin** : overly sentimental _____

   Dictionary definition _____

6. **temerity** : rashness _____

   Dictionary definition _____

7. **incite** : provoke _____

   Dictionary definition _____

8. **commiseration** : pity _____

   Dictionary definition _____

Vocabulary Power continued

9. **ennui** : boredom _____

   Dictionary definition _____

10. **garish** : flashy _____

    Dictionary definition _____

EXERCISE B Word Replacement

Replace the italicized expression with the vocabulary word that best fits.

1. The family of the deceased fireman appreciated the mayor's *expression of sympathy.* _____

2. The leader of the guerrilla fighters was charged with trying to *provoke* an uprising against the government.

   _____

3. "Your total *lack of sensitivity* to the rights of others forces me to give you the longest jail sentence I can,"
   said the judge sternly. _____

4. We were not amused at Peter's *criticism* of the river clean-up committee. _____

5. Laura was amazed at her little brother's *boldness* in asking the football star for his autograph.

   _____

6. Judy decided to *ruthlessly plunder* her kitchen cabinets for chocolate. _____

7. Everyone deals with *a feeling of boredom* during teenage years. _____

8. The signs for businesses along this street are *distressingly bright.* _____

9. Bill presented his opinions in a *forcibly expressed* manner. _____

10. This music is a bit too *weakly sentimental* for me. _____

Vocabulary Power

Lesson 45   Prefixes That Show Quantity or Size

Knowing the meaning of prefixes can help you discover the meanings of unknown words. A large number of prefixes show quantity or size. Some of these prefixes are *macro-, pan-, omni-, oli-, ambi-,* and *poly-.* Be careful, though. Not all words that begin with these letter combinations have the meaning of the prefix. When in doubt, look up the word in a dictionary.

Word List			
ambidextrous	oligarchy	panacea	polyglot
ambivalent	omniscient	panorama	polytheistic
macrocosm	omnivorous		

EXERCISE A   Prefixes

Underline the prefix in each of the ten boldfaced words. Use the clues to answer each question. Then, check the definition of each vocabulary word and write its meaning.

1. **macrocosm:** *kosmos* is the Greek word for "world." Adding the Greek prefix *macro-,* which means "large," to this root creates a word that probably means _____

   Dictionary definition _____

2. **panacea:** The Greek prefix *pan-* is a number prefix that means "all" or "whole." Which diseases do you think that a **panacea** cures? _____

   Dictionary definition _____

3. **panorama:** *Orama* is a Greek root meaning "sight." Affixing the prefix *pan-* creates a word that probably means

   _____

   Dictionary definition _____

4. **omnivorous:** An animal that is carnivorous eats meat, while one that is herbivorous eats plants. If the Latin prefix *omni-* means *all,* what does an **omnivorous** animal eat? _____

   Dictionary definition _____

5. **omniscient:** The root *sciens* comes from the Latin word for "knowing." If someone is **omniscient,** how would you describe him or her? _____

   Dictionary definition _____

6. **oligarchy:** A patriarchy is a social system in which fathers rule as the heads of families. In a matriarchy, mothers are dominant. Since the Greek prefix *olig-, oligo-* means "few," what kind of government would you guess an **oligarchy** is? _____

   Dictionary definition _____

Vocabulary Power *continued*

7. **ambivalent:** *Ambi-* is a Latin prefix that means "both." If someone has **ambivalent** feelings about a subject, what words might describe these feelings? _____

Dictionary definition _____

8. **ambidextrous:** Most people are right-handed, while a small percentage are left-handed. Very few people are **ambidextrous.** What special ability do these people possess? _____

Dictionary definition _____

9. **polyglot:** *Poly-* is a common prefix. It comes from the Greek word for "many." *Glot* comes from the Greek word for "tongue." If a country's population is described as **polyglot,** what does that probably mean?

_____

Dictionary definition _____

10. **polytheistic:** Christianity, Judaism, and Islam are monotheistic religions; Christians, Jews, and Muslims believe in a single deity. Hinduism, on the other hand, is **polytheistic.** How does it differ from the others?

_____

Dictionary definition _____

EXERCISE B Definitions

Answer each question based on your understanding of the boldfaced vocabulary word.

1. Which form of government is the opposite of an **oligarchy?** _____

_____

2. Name an animal that is **omnivorous** and one that is not. _____

_____

3. If a reviewer describes a novel as "a **panorama** of American society in the twentieth century," what qualities might the novel have? _____

_____

4. "I admit that I am **ambivalent** about being nominated for the office of governor," said the crime-busting district attorney, "because...." [Finish the district attorney's sentence.] _____

_____

5. What is one benefit of a country having a **polyglot** population? What is one disadvantage? _____

_____

Vocabulary Power

Lesson 46   Words from Technology

Technology is the source of many new and interesting words in the English language. These words often find their way into everyday usage. In addition, words from technology can be formed in fascinating ways. The words in this lesson are technological words everyone needs to know and understand.

Word List

analog	ergonomics	modem	polymer
bioengineering	facsimile	photoelectric	virtual
digital	laser		

EXERCISE A Definitions

Look up each word in a dictionary and write its meaning.

1. laser _____

2. polymer _____

3. bioengineering _____

4. photoelectric _____

5. modem _____

6. digital _____

7. analog _____

8. facsimile _____

9. ergonomics _____

10. virtual _____

EXERCISE B Sentence Completion

Write the vocabulary word that best completes the sentence.

1. Computer technology is also known as _____ technology because computers use numbers instead of letters to function.

2. Plastic is probably the best-known _____, a class of materials made by linking many small, simple molecules.

3. Where would modern business be today without the ability to transmit e-mail messages and access the Internet easily and quickly using various _____?

4. The designer of our uncomfortable office furniture never studied the science of _____.

Vocabulary Power *continued*

5. The new video arcade features several games in which the experience, while not actually real, is

   _____.

6. Have you heard about these amazing new surgical techniques in which the surgeon uses light, in the form

   of a(n) _____, instead of a knife?

7. My uncle will not own a digital clock because a(n) _____ clock face is much easier to read.

8. For the science fair, we built a propeller based on energy received from the classroom lights and

   transmitted through a(n) _____ cell.

9. To use the fax machine, just insert the paper in the tray and enter the reception number; then, a

   _____ of your document will emerge at the other end.

10. The article predicted that, within ten years, _____ would make possible the growth of

    spare human organs to use for transplants.

EXERCISE C Context Clues

Answer each question based on the context. Use a dictionary if necessary.

1. What is the difference between information expressed in **digital** form and **analog** form? Give examples of

   an instrument or device that represents information in each form. _____

   _____

2. Is a photograph of something a **facsimile** of it? Is a painting? Explain your answers. _____

   _____

3. An acronym is a word like *radar*, made up of the first letters of the original expression, such as **ra**dio

   detecting **a**nd **r**anging. Name two acronyms. What words do their letters represent? _____

   _____

4. Which two words are formed by combining common prefixes that mean "life" and "light," respectively, with

   other words? _____

5. If you were an engineer in charge of designing the interiors of cars, which word represents the field that

   would be most important to you? Why? _____

   _____

EXERCISE D Multiple-Meaning Words

On a separate sheet of paper, create a crossword puzzle using four of the vocabulary words in this lesson. This activity challenges you to show two different meanings for each of the four words. Write four "down" clues and four "across" clues for the same four words, but with different meanings. Then, trade puzzles with a partner.

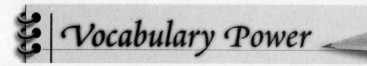

Vocabulary Power

Review: Unit 12

EXERCISE

Circle the letter of the word that can best replace the italicized expression.

1. Brad believed that sending roses was the *cure-all* for Jenna's annoyance at him.
   a. denigration   **b.** panacea   **c.** temerity   **d.** polymer

2. The date A.D. 476 is one that marks the fall of the Roman Empire and the *plundering* of the Imperial City by the Germanic tribes.
   a. pillage   **b.** panorama   **c.** panacea   **d.** polymer

3. To connect to the Internet, your computer must be equipped with a *device that transmits data over the telephone lines.*
   a. oligarchy   **b.** facsimile   **c.** laser   **d.** modem

4. We had a breathtaking *total view* of the battlefield from the observation tower.
   a. panorama   **b.** denigration   **c.** macrocosm   **d.** oligarchy

5. Rachel's feelings about attending the game were *mixed;* she wanted to go, yet she also wanted to visit with her cousins from Illinois.
   a. maudlin   **b.** digital   **c.** ambivalent   **d.** omnivorous

6. Latorry felt that Rosemont's volleyball uniforms were *tasteless and showy*, with their gold trim, green letters, and baggy white-and-orange shorts.
   a. photoelectric   **b.** maudlin   **c.** polyglot   **d.** garish

7. Ben demonstrated his *insensitivity* when he walked by without even glancing at our display.
   a. denigration   **b.** callousness   **c.** temerity   **d.** commiseration

8. For his birthday, my little brother wants a set of those new *near*-reality goggles.
   a. vehement   **b.** digital   **c.** virtual   **d.** ambivalent

9. Many kitchen products and gadgets are now designed using the principles of *the science of human interaction with machines.*
   a. bioengineering   **b.** macrocosm   **c.** ergonomics   **d.** oligarchy

10. The speaker tried to *provoke* the protesters to action.
    a. incite   **b.** pillage   **c.** allude   **d.** laser

Vocabulary Power

Test: Unit 12

PART A

Circle the letter of the word that best completes each sentence.

1. To understand the _____, stated the philosopher, one must study the microcosm thoroughly.
   a. macrocosm   b. commiseration   c. oligarchy   d. analog

2. The candidate for governor promised she would not engage in negative campaigning and the _____ of her opponent.
   a. commiseration   b. facsimile   c. denigration   d. callousness

3. The eagle attacked the gopher with the speed of a lightning bolt and the concentration of a _____.
   a. panacea   b. polyglot   c. laser   d. modem

4. The lawyer for the defendant asked the judge not to _____ to her client's previous conviction for robbery.
   a. allude   b. incite   c. pillage   d. denigrate

5. It took great _____ for Lupe to enter the contest without the necessary credentials.
   a. oligarchy   b. temerity   c. commiseration   d. denigration

6. Thanks to its outstanding research in _____, the university received generous funding for its artificial-hip manufacturing technique.
   a. bioengineering   b. commiseration   c. ergonomics   d. oligarchy

7. Ricky's dog Caleb is the most _____ creature I've ever seen; in addition to plants and animals, he also eats shoes, books, pencils, furniture, sports equipment, and radios!
   a. garish   b. maudlin   c. omniscient   d. omnivorous

8. If you put your hand between the _____ cell and the light bulb, the little mechanical horse will stop jumping around.
   a. garish   b. polyglot   c. photoelectric   d. vehement

9. Monique felt strong _____ for the earthquake victims.
   a. temerity   b. commiseration   c. denigration   d. callousness

10. Claiming that political power should always be concentrated in the few, the debater defended the system of government known as _____.
    a. denigration   b. pillage   c. oligarchy   d. panorama

PART B

Circle the letter of the word that best answers the question.

1. Which quality would be *least* valuable in a good friend?
   a. commiseration   b. ergonomics   c. temerity   d. callousness

Vocabulary Power continued

2. In which activity would being ambidextrous be the most helpful?
   a. playing basketball **b.** swimming **c.** playing chess **d.** reading

3. A wall clock with hour, minute, and second hands is an example of what kind of device?
   a. digital **b.** analog **c.** omniscient **d.** omnivorous

4. Which of the following activities might be described as maudlin?
   a. getting an A on a history quiz **c.** crying over the death of a baby rabbit
   b. applying for a part-time job **d.** cheering at a sports event

5. Which word would you most likely use to describe a meeting of the United Nations General Assembly?
   a. garish **b.** ambidextrous **c.** virtual **d.** polyglot

6. Which word would you most likely use to describe a reproduction of a photograph?
   a. denigration **b.** callousness **c.** facsimile **d.** pillage

7. What kind of watch do many athletes use?
   a. digital **b.** vehement **c.** polymer **d.** garish

8. Antibiotics are often considered a _____.
   a. panacea **b.** panorama **c.** bioengineering **d.** commiseration

9. Guerrillas try to do what to change a crowd into a mob?
   a. allude to it **b.** pillage it **c.** incite it **d.** analog it

10. Appearing at a school dance with blue hair, black makeup, green fur earmuffs, several tattoos, and ice skates could best be described as what kind of fashion statement?
    a. photoelectric **b.** garish **c.** maudlin **d.** ambidextrous

11. "Maybe yes, maybe no" is an answer that implies what kind of feeling?
    a. a vehement one **b.** an omniscient one **c.** a polytheistic one **d.** an ambivalent one

12. If an army of barbarians appeared outside the castle in which you lived screaming, waving their spears, and throwing rocks at the castle, what would you think they had in mind?
    a. to show their commiseration **c.** to pillage your home
    b. to deliver a panacea **d.** to build a laser

13. What is the best way to connect to the Internet?
    a. with a modem **b.** with a laser **c.** with a polymer **d.** with a photoelectric cell

14. Someone interested in designing new kinds of plastics for soft-drink bottles would have to be knowledgeable in what field?
    a. laser technology **b.** polymer science **c.** bioengineering **d.** ergonomics

15. What reaction might you have to an arsonist who has set a raging fire?
    a. a maudlin one **b.** a vehement one **c.** a polyglot one **d.** a garish one

abstemious ab stē´mē əs

abyss ə bis´

accessible ak ses´ə bəl

acrimonious ak´rə mō´nē əs

acute ə kūt´

adamant ad´ə mənt

adhere ad hēr´

adroit ə droit´

adversary ad´vər ser´ē

aesthetic es thet´ik

affable af´ə bəl

agnostic ag nos´tik

allude ə lood´

ambidextrous am´bi deks´trəs

ambivalent am biv´ə lənt

ameliorate a mēl´yə rāt´

amoral ā môr´əl

amorphous ə môr´fəs

amphibian am fib´ē ən

analog an´ə log

annihilate ə nī´ə lāt´

antagonize an tag´ə nīz´

antibiotic an´tē bī ot´ik

anticlimax an´ti klī´maks

antipathy an tip´ə thē

apprise ə prīz´

astral as´trəl

astronomer əs tron´ə mər

audacious ô dā´shəs

austere ôs tēr´

avarice av´ər is

bioengineering bī´ō en´ji nēr´ing

bionic bī on´ik

biopsy bi´op´sē

blighted blīt´id

boor boor

bumptious bump´shəs

burgeoning bur´jən ing

cajole kə jōl´

callousness kal´əs nəs

cartography kär tog´rə fē

caustic kôs´tik

cheerful chēr´fəl

churlish chur´lish

coerce kō urs´

coherent kō hēr´ənt

collusion kə loo´zhən

commemorate kə mem´ə rāt´

commiseration kə miz´ə rā´shən

complacent kəm plā´sənt

conciliatory kən sil´ē ə tôr´ē

condolence kən dō´ləns

congenial kən jēn´yəl

conjecture kən jek´chər

connoisseur kon´ə sur´

conspiratorial kən spir´ə tôr´ē əl

constraint kən strānt´

contention kən ten´shən

contiguous kən tig´ū əs

contraindicate kon´trə in´di kāt´

contravene kon´trə vēn´

converge kən vurj´

convivial kən viv´ē əl

copious kō´pē əs

copiously kō´pē əs lē

counterbalance koun´tər bal´əns

countermand koun´tər mand´

credibility kred´ə bil´ə tē

creditable kred´i tə bəl

credo krē´dō

criterion krī tēr´ē ən

cursory kur´sər ē

curt kurt

debacle di bä´kəl

deference def´ər əns

deftly deft´lē

delude di lood´

deluge del´ūj

demagogue dem´ə gog´

demographic dē´mə graf´ik

denigration den´ə grā´shən

depravity di prav´ə tē

depreciate di prē´shē āt´

derisive di rī´siv

derogatory di rog´ə tôr´ē

despicable des´pi kə bəl

despondent di spon´dənt

detrimental de´trə ment´əl

diffident dif´ə dənt

digital dij´it əl

digress   di gres´

diligently   dil´ə jənt lē

disconcerting   dis´kən surt´ing

disconsolate   dis kon´sə lit

discredit   dis kred´it

disillusion   dis´i lo͞o´zhən

disparaging   dis par´ij ing

dispassionate   dis pash´ə nit

dissemble   di sem´bəl

diverge   di vurj´

dogmatic   dôg mat´ik

doleful   dōl´fəl

dolorous   dō´lər əs

dramatization   dram´ə ti zā´shən

droll   drōl

duress   do͞o res´

edification   ed´ə fi kā´shən

effluent   ef´lo͞o ənt

egregious   i grē´jəs

elucidate   i lo͞o´sə dāt´

elude   i lo͞od´

emulate   em´yə lāt´

endemic   en dem´ik

endurance   en door´əns

enigma   i nig´mə

enmity   en´mə tē

epicenter   ep´i sen´tər

epidemic   ep´ə dem´ik

epidermis   ep´ə dur´mis

epigone   ep´ə gon´

epigram   ep´ə gram´

epiphany   i pif´ə nē

epistle   i pis´əl

epitome   i pit´ə mē

equinox   ēk´wə noks´

ergonomics   ur gə nom´iks

erudite   er´yo͞o dīt´

estrange   es trānj´

ethereal   i thēr´ē əl

evanescent   ev´ə nes´ənt

evocative   i vok´ə tiv

exacerbate   ig zas´ər bāt´

exhort   ig zôrt´

exotic   ig zot´ik

expedient   iks pē´dē ənt

extenuating   iks ten´ū ā´ting

extol   eks tōl´

extrapolate   iks trap´ə lāt´

extravagant   iks trav´ə gənt

facsimile   fak sim´ə lē

faculty   fak´əl tē

fanaticism   fə nat´ə siz´əm

farce   färs

fatuous   fach´o͞o əs

fecund   fē´kənd

feign   fān

fiasco   fē as´kō

fluctuate   fluk´cho͞o āt´

foray   fôr´ā

frivolous   friv´ə ləs

furtive   fur´tiv

gallant   gal´ənt (also gə lant´ depending on definition)

garish   gār´ish

garrulous   gar´ə ləs

gauche   gōsh

generic   jə ner´ik

genesis   jen´ə sis

genocide   jen´ə sīd´

genre   zhän´rə

genteel   jen tēl´

grandeur   gran´jər

grandiose   gran´dē ōs´

graphology   graf ol´ə jē

gregarious   gri gār´ē əs

gullible   gul´ə bəl

hamper   ham´pər

hemisphere   hem´is fēr´

heterogeneous   het´ər ə jē´nē əs

hinder   hin´dər

homogeneous   hō´mə jē´nē əs

ignoble   ig nō´bəl

illumination   i lo͞o´mə nā´shən

illusionist   i lo͞o´zhə nist

illusive   i lo͞o´siv

illusory   i lo͞o´sər ē

illustrious   i lus´trē əs

immaculate   i mak´yə lit

immemorial   im´ə môr´ē əl

immutable   i mū´tə bəl

impartial   im pär´shəl

impel im pel´

imperturbable im´pər tur´bə bəl

impervious im pur´vē əs

impetus im´pə təs

impinge im pinj´

implausible im plô´zə bəl

incite in sīt´

incongruous in kong´grōō əs

incredulous in krej´ə ləs

index in´deks

indigenous in dij´ə nəs

indiscriminate in dis krim´ə nit

ineffable in ef´ə bəl

inept i nept´

ineptly i nept´lē

infallible in fal´ə bəl

ingenious in jēn´yəs

ingenuous in jen´ū əs

inherent in hēr´ənt

inimitable in im´ə tə bəl

innate i nāt´

inscrutable in skrōō´tə bəl

insipid in sip´id

intangible in tan´jə bəl

inter in tur´

interlude in´tər lōōd´

intermediary in´tər mē´dē er´ē

intersperse in´tər spurs´

intrepid in trep´id

invigorating in vig´ə rāt´ing

irrelevant i rel´ə vənt

kindle kind´əl

kumquat kum´kwot

laceration las´ə rā´shən

laconic lə kon´ik

languish lang´gwish

laser lā´zər

laudable lô´də bəl

lavish lav´ish

legibility lej ə bil´ə tē

lenient lē´nē ənt

leverage lev´ər ij

levitation lev´ə tā´shən

levity lev´ə tē

liable lī´ə bəl

liberal lib´ər əl

listless list´lis

loquacious lō kwā´shəs

lucent lōō´sənt

lucid lōō´sid

lucubration lōō´kyə brā´shən

ludicrous lōō´də krəs

lunacy lōō´nə sē

lunatic lōō´nə tik

lurid loor´id

macabre mə kä´brə

macrocosm mak´rə koz´əm

magnanimous mag nan´ə məs

malcontent mal´kən tent´

maudlin môd´lin

megalomania meg´ə lō mā´nē ə

memoir mem´wär

memorabilia mem´ər ə bil´ē ə

memorandum mem´ə ran´dəm

mercenary mur´sə ner´ē

metamorphosis met´ə môr´fə sis

methodical mə thod´i kəl

microbe mī´krōb

mirth murth

modem mō´dəm

mollify mol´ə fī´

mundane mun dān´

muse mūz

necessary nes´ə ser´ē

negate ni gāt´

nocturnal nok turn´əl

nonentity non en´tə tē

notoriety nō´tə rī´ə tē

nullify nul´ə fī´

obdurate ob´dər it

obfuscation ob fus kā´shən

oblivious ə bliv´ē əs

obstreperous əb strep´ər əs

oligarchy ol´ə gär´kē

omniscient om nish´ənt

omnivorous om niv´ər əs

opportune op´ər tōōn´

opprobrium ə prō´brē əm

ostensible os ten´sə bəl

ostentatious os´tən tā´shəs

ostracize os′trə sīz′

outlandish out lan′dish

paltry pôl′trē

panacea pan′ə sē′ə

pandemic pan dem′ik

panorama pan′ə ram′ə

parch pärch

parry par′ē

paucity pô′sə tē

penance pen′əns

penitent pen′ə tənt

pensive pen′siv

pernicious pər nish′əs

pertinent purt′ən ənt

phosphorescent fos′fə res′ənt

photoelectric fō′tō i lek′trik

photogenic fō′tə jen′ik

photograph fō′tə graf′

photosensitive fō tə sen′sə tiv

photosynthesis fō′tə sin′thə sis

piety pī′ə tē

pillage pil′ij

piquant pē′kənt

pithy pith′ē

placid plas′id

plaintive plān′tiv

poignant poin′yənt

polyglot pol′ē glot′

polymer pol′i mər

polytheistic pol′ē thē is′tik

precept prē′sept

preclude pri klōōd′

predilection pred′əl ek′shən

predominance pri dom′ə nəns

prehensile prē hen′sil

privation prī vā′shən

procrastination prō kras′tə nā′shən

procure prə kyoor′

prodigious prə dij′əs

prognosis prog nō′sis

proliferation prō lif′ə rā′shən

propensity prə pen′sə tē

propitious prə pish′əs

prosaic prō zā′ik

proscribe prō skrīb′

quagmire kwag′mīr′

quandary kwon′dər ē

ravage rav′ij

raze rāz

reciprocate ri sip′rə kāt′

refulgent ri ful′jənt

regale ri gāl′

reprehensible rep′ri hen′sə bəl

reproach ri prōch′

respite res′pit

resplendent ri splen′dənt

retroactive ret′rō ak′tiv

retrofit ret′rō fit′

retrograde ret′rə grād′

retrogress ret′rə gres′

retrospective ret′rə spek′tiv

reverie rev′ər ē

revive ri vīv′

saunter sôn′tər

scintillating sint′əl ā′ting

seismograph sīz′mə graf′

sequester si kwes′tər

severe sə vēr′

sluggish slug′ish

smirk smurk

solicitous sə lis′ə təs

steadfastly sted′fast′lē

stoic stō′ik

subjugate sub′jə gāt′

sublunary sub′loo ner′ē

subservient səb sur′vē ənt

subterranean sub′tə rā′nē ən

superficial sōō′pər fish′əl

superfluous soo pur′flōō əs

supplant sə plant′

surfeited sur′fit id

sustenance sus′tə nəns

symbiosis sim′bī ō′sis

tactful takt′fəl

tangential tan jen′chəl

tangible tan′jə bəl

tawdry tôd′rē

temerity tə mer′ə tē

temper tem′pər

tenet ten′it

tenuous   ten´ū əs

tenure   ten´yər

terrace   ter´is

terrarium   tə rār´ē əm

terrestrial   tə res´trē əl

territorial   ter´ə tôr´ē əl

thwart   thwôrt

tome   tōm

topography   tə pog´rə fē

torpor   tôr´pər

transcend   tran send´

transfigure   trans fig´yər

transfix   trans fiks´

transfusion   trans fū´zhən

transgress   trans gres´

transient   tran´shənt

transition   tran zish´ən

translucent   trans lōō´sənt

transmogrify   trans mog´rə fī´

transmute   trans mūt´

transpire   tran spīr´

transpose   trans pōz´

transverse   trans vurs´

unfathomable   un fath´əm ə bəl

unkempt   un kempt´

unobtrusive   un´əb trōō´siv

unprecedented   un pres´ə den´tid

unpretentious   un´pri ten´shəs

unsavory   un sā´vər ē

urbane   ur bān´

vehement   vē´ə mənt

venture   ven´chər

vex   veks

viability   vī´ə bil´ə tē

viable   vī´ə bəl

virtual   vur´chōō əl

vitality   vī tal´ə tē

vivacious   vi vā´shəs

vivid   viv´id

voluminous   və lōō´mə nəs

whimsical   hwim´zi kəl

writhe   rīth